# Historians and Race

# BLACKS IN THE DIASPORA

Darlene Clark Hine, John McCluskey, Jr.,
and David Barry Gaspar   GENERAL EDITORS

# Historians and Race

AUTOBIOGRAPHY

AND THE

WRITING OF HISTORY

Edited by Paul A. Cimbala
and Robert F. Himmelberg

INDIANA UNIVERSITY PRESS
BLOOMINGTON AND INDIANAPOLIS

THE PAPER USED IN THIS PUBLICATION MEETS THE MINIMUM REQUIREMENTS OF
AMERICAN NATIONAL STANDARD FOR INFORMATION SCIENCES—PERMANENCE OF PAPER
FOR PRINTED LIBRARY MATERIALS, ANSI Z39.48-1984.

MANUFACTURED IN THE UNITED STATES OF AMERICA

LIBRARY OF CONGRESS CATALOGING-IN-PUBLICATION DATA
HISTORIANS AND RACE : AUTOBIOGRAPHY AND THE WRITING OF HISTORY /
  EDITED BY PAUL A. CIMBALA AND ROBERT F. HIMMELBERG.
      P.    CM. — (BLACKS IN THE DIASPORA)
PAPERS FROM SYMPOSIA HELD AT FORDHAM UNIVERSITY.
INCLUDES INDEX.
  ISBN 0–253–33235–4 (CL : ALK. PAPER). — ISBN 0–253–21101–8 (PA :
ALK. PAPER)
    1. HISTORIANS—UNITED STATES—BIOGRAPHY—CONGRESSES.   2. AFRO-
AMERICANS—HISTORIOGRAPHY—CONGRESSES.   3. UNITED STATES—RACE
RELATIONS—CONGRESSES.   4. AFRO-AMERICANS—CIVIL RIGHTS—CONGRESSES.
5. CIVIL RIGHTS MOVEMENTS—UNITED STATES—HISTORY—20TH CENTURY—
CONGRESSES.   I. CIMBALA, PAUL A. (PAUL ALAN).   II. HIMMELBERG, ROBERT F.
III. SERIES.
E175.45.H567    1996
973'.007202—DC20                                    96–24749
    1   2   3   4   5   01   00   99   98   97   96

TO THE MEMORY OF OUR COLLEAGUE AND FRIEND

George J. Gill *(1927–1995)*

# Contents

GEORGE B. TINDALL
   1. Jumping Jim Crow
          1

LEON F. LITWACK
   2. The Making of a Historian
             15

DAN T. CARTER
   3. Reflections of a Reconstructed White Southerner
                         33

DARLENE CLARK HINE
   4. Reflections on Race and Gender Systems
               51

DAVID LEVERING LEWIS
   5. From Eurocentrism to Polycentrism
             66

Contents

## Acknowledgments

The editors wish to thank the Reverend Joseph A. O'Hare, President of Fordham University, for encouraging us to stage the three symposia that produced the essays published in this volume. He and the Reverend Gerard Reedy, S.J., formerly Dean of Fordham College, Dean of the Liberal Arts Faculty, and Vice President for Academic Affairs of Fordham University, currently President of the College of the Holy Cross in Worcester, Massachusetts, graciously and enthusiastically supported our efforts. They both reminded us that the Jesuits remain committed to social justice and the education of the whole individual by doing what appears to be one of the most difficult things university administrators must do in these times of problematic budgets—provide funds on short notice for a faculty project. Dr. Mary Powers, presently Professor of Sociology at Fordham University, in her former capacity as Dean of the Graduate School of Arts and Sciences supported our belief in the importance of the humanistic and even idiosyncratic approach to a major social concern by finding funds in her strained budget to contribute to the support of the first of our symposia. The Graduate School continued to support our efforts after

Dr. Powers returned to teaching and Robert Himmelberg assumed the position of dean. On all occasions, the student organization American Age set aside substantial resources to bring our speakers to campus; it deserves recognition for its contribution to responsible student programming. Also, undergraduate and graduate students in the History Department's chapter of Phi Alpha Theta took care of essential tasks that contributed to the success of the symposia, as did Thomas Lombardi, Paul Cimbala's graduate assistant, for the most recent event. Maureen Hanratty, the executive secretary of the Graduate School of Arts and Sciences, and Barbara Costa, the secretary of the Department of History, helped to keep the symposia on track by calmly resolving all sorts of tedious administrative problems. Finally, the editors would like to thank our contributors. They are delightful colleagues whose exemplary expressions of scholarship reflect the joy and the commitment they bring to their work.

*Acknowledgments*

## Introduction

This volume has its origins in Fordham University's quest to find ways to revive interest among its undergraduates in the continuing struggle for racial justice. During the late 1980s, the Reverend Joseph O'Hare, S.J., the university's president, issued a call to the university community to devise creative ways to rekindle an awareness of the work and the goals of the men and women of good will who had rallied to Martin Luther King, Jr.'s call to action. The editors, members of Fordham University's Department of History, responded by organizing three symposia on scholarship and race in America that generated the papers now published in this collection.

In choosing this approach, we hoped to go beyond just another series of lectures that presented significant historical content but failed to stimulate an emotional response in our students. Certainly, we wished to correct misperceptions about race by giving our audiences sound scholarship. We were concerned that our students might have lost interest in the ongoing struggle for racial justice because they had come to assume that the civil rights movement had either accomplished all that it could or that its present agenda had propelled it beyond legitimate goals. We were especially disturbed by the negative impact that the new rhetoric of separatism and racial hatred might have on our students, students whose only contact with the goals of an earlier movement primarily concerned with equal rights and desegregation might be in one or two lectures of an introductory history class. Presentations that provided proper historical context could help address these concerns, but we both believed that the human interest generated by autobiography would be the most effective route for achieving our ends. We concluded that lectures presented by prominent scholars who reflected on both their professional and personal commitments to understanding the problem of race in America would be not only most appropriate but exciting as well.

In recruiting participants for our symposia, we approached internationally recognized historians who represent the generational, regional, and racial richness of the profession. We specifically asked them to reflect upon their careers and how their personal experiences might have influenced their approach to scholarship. The initial responses were interesting. The contributors were delighted to have an opportunity to address our questions, especially those who candidly admitted that they had never thought much about why they did what they did or what purpose their work might have beyond the usual scholarly ends. As David Levering Lewis notes in his essay, "A curious deficit of introspection is commonplace among professional historians." We were happy to provide the contributors with an opportunity to address that deficit, as well as our larger hope that history, as Darlene Clark Hine writes, might provide "a way for understanding events that increasingly [make] little sense." We believe the fruits of our contributors' efforts are worth sharing with students, scholars, and interested readers beyond the gates of our own university.

Introduction

# 1. Jumping Jim Crow

George B. Tindall is William Rand Kenan, Jr., Professor
Emeritus at the University of North Carolina at Chapel
Hill. He earned his B.A. at Furman University in 1942,
his M.A. at the University of North Carolina at Chapel
Hill in 1948, and his Ph.D. at the same institution in
1951. Prior to his appointment at Chapel Hill in 1958,
he taught at Eastern Kentucky State College, the University of Mississippi, and Louisiana State University. A former president of the Southern Historical Association, he
has been a Guggenheim Fellow, a member of the Institute
for Advanced Study, a Social Science Research Council Fellow, and a Fulbright Professor at the University of Vienna.
Professor Tindall's book The Emergence of the New
South, 1913–1945 (1967) won numerous awards,
among them the Charles S. Sydnor Award of the Southern
Historical Association and the Lillian E. Smith Award of
the Southern Regional Council. Among his other publications are South Carolina Negroes, 1877–1900
(1952); The Disruption of the Solid South (1972),
the Eugenia Dorothy Blount Lamar Memorial Lectures at
Mercer University; The Persistent Tradition in New
South Politics (1975), the Walter Lynwood Fleming
Lectures at Louisiana State University; and The Ethnic
Southerners (1976). Professor Tindall is also author of

the best-selling textbook America: A Narrative History, first published in 1984, and recently published Natives and Newcomers: Ethnic Southerners and Southern Ethnics. He continues to explore the American South's distinctive place in United States history.

---

Come, listen all you gals and boys,
Ise just from Tuckyhoe; I'm goin to
sing a little song,
My name's Jim Crow. Weel about and
turn about and do jis so, Eb'ry time I
wheel about I jump Jim Crow. [1]

---

Jim Crow had a strange career in show business long before he took to riding trains and going to school. It began with the song just quoted, from one of the infinite variations, and the dance routine that went with it. In those days, Jim Crow may have been a lot more fun than he got to be later, but he also had a lot to do with fixing in the American tradition the clownish stereotype of Sambo, the old-time darkey who was just as happy as if he had good sense. The Jim Crow routine was not the first blackface act, but it was the first to become a public sensation—both here and abroad.

Thomas Dartmouth "Daddy" Rice, a white native of New York City, first brought the act to the stage. While on tour with a stage company in 1828 or thereabouts, he encountered the original, an old black man with a right shoulder deformed and brought up high, one leg gnarled and crooked, who exploited his handicaps to jump Jim Crow. Rice copied the performance, added his own flourishes, put it on as a between-acts routine, and its success propelled him from obscurity to fame and fortune. Jim Crow himself, however, became an invisible man. Strangely, for somebody so notorious, his identity remains a mystery, and his very existence has been called into question. Accounts differ as

Jumping Jim Crow

to his home town, variously given as Louisville, Cincinnati, Pittsburgh, St. Louis, New Orleans, and Charleston, most often as one of the first two.[2]

The spread of acts like Daddy Rice's led soon to the invention of the American minstrel show. The first, Dan Emmett's "Virginia Minstrels," was the hasty contrivance of a few performers down on their luck who took to the New York stage in February 1843.[3] The inspiration for the name apparently was a group called the "Tyrolean Minstrels," who had recently visited the city. In adopting the name they gave an entirely new meaning to the old medieval word for traveling performers. A standard format soon jelled. The interlocutor presided, as straight man for the comic end men, Tambo and Bones. Then came the olio, a series of song and dance acts topped off by the strutting "walkaround" or "cakewalk," and finally an "Ethiopian Opera," often a take-off on some classic such as *Othello*.

Never long on realism, owing more to the comic traditions of Europe than to Afro-American culture, the shows in some ways humanized blacks. Black slaves might have been puttin' on ole Massa much of the time. Blackface minstrels were puttin' him down. Tambo and Bones were forever one up on the white interlocutor. And the show of rank humbled no doubt accounted for much of the minstrels' popularity, entirely aside from the racial context.

Minstrel shows ultimately provided an entrée into show business for blacks, if at some cost to their dignity, and evolved into latter-day variety shows, vaudeville, and even burlesque. Without stretching the truth too far, one could make a case for Jim Crow as the progenitor of American popular entertainment. Certainly he deeply influenced the way it went.

Well before the Civil War, Jim Crow's name became synonymous with "Negro," especially one of the rustic and comic sort. In *Uncle Tom's Cabin*, for instance, a character referred to Topsy as "a rather funny specimen in the Jim Crow line."[4]

3

*George B. Tindall*

Eventually, by the turn of the century, the name mutated into an eponym for segregation. Jim Crow became an adjective and a verb, as well as a noun. Along the way the name attached itself to a Jim Crow comb, to substandard railroad ties, to a bending machine for rails (presumably because of Jim Crow's bent body), to a planing machine that had blades cutting both ways (probably a reference to his dance). These soon vanished, embalmed in reference books.[5]

Even Jim Crow's career in show business sank below the horizons of living memory; but the comic blacks perpetrated by the minstrels lived on, preserved if modified in their successors: vaudeville shows, motion pictures, radio, and television.

For well over a century, then, Americans were jumping Jim Crow to one tune or another. It was into such a world that most Southerners, indeed most Americans, were born during the first half of the twentieth century.

The idea of these essays, as I understand it, is for each contributor to give a personal view of the history of race relations. I propose to revisit the strange career of Jim Crow, but less the book of that title than my own first book entitled *South Carolina Negroes, 1877–1900* (published in 1952 and derived from my dissertation, completed in the summer of 1950) and how it was I arrived at that subject.

What follows, then, will be something like the title of a Frank Sullivan story, "The Night the Old Nostalgia Burned Down." It may be more personal than the planners bargained for. After putting these remarks together I realized that I had used with awkward frequency the perpendicular pronoun, by which I mean the first person singular subjective. But I can also be objective, I hope—as well as possessive.

In the world of my up-country South Carolina childhood, I suppose I took many things, including Jim Crow, as given, just the way things were and always had been. My family was in the retail hardware business but still not far removed from the land on either side. And I was the first on either side of the family to make it through college.

Just what influences first led me to a dawning awareness and curiosity about the racial mores of that world is hard to say. My colleague Joel Williamson has argued that just growing up in South Carolina was enough, especially in the first half of the twentieth century. He has a point, I think.

My earliest memory of any awareness of the subject is one of overhearing arguments among fellow seven-year-olds about whether Al Smith or Herbert Hoover would put blacks in the White House, although "blacks" was not the word they used. Aside from that, the earliest memory that has lodged in my mind is the example of a fourth-grade teacher named Laura Butler lecturing the class about an incident in which passing black children had been pushed off the sidewalk after school. Their parents, she informed us, were citizens and paid taxes like our own parents. They had as much right to the sidewalk, therefore, as anybody else.

I had neither been in nor witnessed the incident, I hasten to add, but looking back on it now, I find it an intriguing reversal of old Reconstruction stories about blacks pushing whites off the sidewalks. One wonders if the fact of the matter may have been that those old stories were, more often than not, inversions of the facts. Aside from that, I suspect that the work of the old Commission on Interracial Cooperation somehow touched me indirectly—and perhaps touched Laura Butler—in ways I shall never know, and that somehow either a social gospel message, or simply a foundation of values, filtered through a conventional religious upbringing, however backslidden a Baptist I may have become since.

Somewhere along the way, certainly before high school, I became a newspaper junkie and a current events buff and thus a member of the group from which many if not most historians are drawn—aside from musty antiquarians. And I remember being startled one day in 1938 by an obituary

_____ 5

George B. Tindall

of Thomas E. Miller, a black man who had been a congressman from the state as late as the 1890s. Actually, Miller was very light in color, and the uninhibited white press of his day gave him the nickname "Canary Bird" Miller.

Our lives are filled with serendipity, and some of us have more luck than any of us probably deserves. It was much later that I came to realize how unusual it was, in that state and that time, to grow up where there were good schools, even for whites. Lingering backwardness even had redeeming features. Greenville High School was still offering history, every year, in surveys that reached from ancient times to modern America. The school was so backward it still offered four years of Latin. My Latin, I confess, has long since evaporated, but I am persuaded that my grasp of English benefited from early exposure to an inflected language.

Sterling High, for blacks, was something else again. I learned only later that, a decade before I entered public high school, there had not been a public high school for blacks in Greenville, just a poverty-stricken private academy. Sterling stressed vocational training, at what level is suggested by the cooking classes, which at the time had to use wood stoves. Requests for foreign language classes by students looking toward college were said to have been greeted with some amusement at a meeting of white teachers. This was what passed at the time for "separate but equal" facilities, yet a segregated high school in those days was an advance over no high school at all. Sterling's best-known alumnus, by the way, is a man named Jesse Jackson, who was not yet born when I was in high school.[6]

I was only vaguely aware of Sterling, but also convinced that something was wrong. I chose, therefore, as the topic for a senior term paper the subject of "Negro Education." It may seem an ambitious topic, but few self-respecting high schoolers need more than ten pages to exhaust any subject. The main point was that there were inequities and that it was just not fair. So far as I know, time has mercifully left in existence no copy of that paper.

We had in that school, too, a teacher of history who was one of the two most memorable instructors I had there. The other was an English teacher who had the oddball hobby of collecting the names of people born in 1809. The history teacher was J. Mauldin Lesesne, later president of Erskine College. His course in South Carolina history, I recall, gave me for the first time some notion of the world of scholarship. Or maybe it was a world of obsession. He had a passion for collecting at least the title of every book ever published having to do with the state's history. He also had an urge to identify every South Carolinian in the *Dictionary of American Biography*, then a fairly recent publication. In lieu of another assignment, he set four of us to scanning the pages, looking for the South Carolinians. Ever since then I've been astonished at students who manage to get to college without ever having heard of the *DAB*—occasionally even a new graduate student manages not to know about it.

During undergraduate years at Furman University, I went astray and fancied myself an English major. College was followed by a lengthy stay in the Pacific, courtesy of the Air Force, but after eight months on a godforsaken mid-Pacific atoll, Canton Island, I sat it out at Hickam Field, my missions pursued on the Honolulu rapid transit system—followed by a workout in officer candidate school.

There one of my classmates was black. This first experience with token integration occurred, incidentally, at Maxwell Field, just outside Montgomery, Alabama, ten years before Rosa Parks set off the civil rights movement there by refusing to give up her bus seat.

We were integrated at Maxwell Field in every way but one. All of us bunked six to a room except the one black classmate, Cecil Poole, who had a room all to himself—and the cleaning of it. Poole is now in San Francisco, a judge on the Ninth Circuit Court of Appeals. I later learned from John Hope Franklin, dean of black historians, that at precisely the time Poole and I were out at Maxwell, he was in Montgomery at the state archives having his first experience with

7

George B. Tindall

an integrated Southern research facility. Integrated probably because it had never occurred to anybody that a black historian might turn up some day.

Finally a civilian again, I fetched up at the University of North Carolina at Chapel Hill in the spring of 1946 as a graduate student in English; but I grew restless in that role and returned in the summer as a history major, working under Fletcher M. Green.

The serendipity held out. Somewhere in my mental data bank had lodged something from that state history class in high school. It was something that I suppose in that time and place a more cautious teacher than J. M. Lesesne might have avoided. In the South Carolina Constitutional Convention of 1895, staged by "Pitchfork Ben" Tillman to disfranchise black voters, Lesesne told us, a member had moved to change the legal definition of Negro from a person with at least one-eighth black ancestry to a person with *any* black ancestry.

At that point, former Congressman George Tillman, Ben's older brother, objected on the grounds that such a change would involve families in his district who had a touch of black ancestry (he said "Negro blood"), but were accepted in white society. To the further consternation of the delegates Tillman argued that probably not a single pure Caucasian sat in the convention. All, he claimed, had colored ancestors, not necessarily Negro but from one of the colored races. He proposed to set the definition at one-fourth, but it stayed at one-eighth.[7]

Still haunted by that revelation, I decided, and Fletcher Green agreed, that the convention would make a suitable thesis topic. In 1947, while I was working on it, Vernon Lane Wharton's pioneering dissertation, *The Negro in Mississippi, 1865–1890*, appeared in print and—Eureka![8] I had found my own dissertation topic, one into which I could incorporate my thesis and try to do for South Carolina what Wharton had done for Mississippi, except that, given Alrutheus A. Taylor's study of *The Negro in South Carolina during* the *Reconstruction*, I decided to pick up where Taylor left off and go on to the end of the century.⁹ It was in the post-Reconstruction years, as the black sociologist E. Franklin Frazier had put it, "that the pattern of race relations in the South was established . . . that the Negro was disfranchised through state constitutions; that discrepancies in educational facilities and the system of racial segregation known as Jim Crow were established by law in the Southern states."¹⁰

My purpose, like Wharton's, was to attempt a panorama of black life in that period, which saw the origins of what Wharton had called the new modus vivendi of race relations: the patterns of disfranchisement, segregation, and economic dependency.

One measure of the distance we have come since those days is the trouble one would have now in recapturing the sense of excitement that came from discovering that the age of segregation dated from a good bit later than remote antiquity, that there were in fact living people who could remember earlier times, a point driven home to me by a conversation with an elderly black pharmacist who remembered when Charleston's opera house, The Academy of Music, was first segregated just after the turn of the century. He never went there again, he said.

The conversation took place about the time Allan Nevins was reinventing oral history. If I had just had a notion of the concept and a tape recorder, it might have been a more fruitful interview. Actually, I was disappointed because I failed to pick up new leads on the nursing school my interviewee's father had founded. Mainly, I'm afraid it seemed to prove the historians' conventional wisdom that memory is fallible and not a useful source. He was not even sure what year it had happened, but it was at a performance of *Madama Butterfly* in either 1903 or 1905—dates which neatly bracket the year of the premiere in Milan: 1904.

By the time of that interview, the National Association for the Advancement of Colored People had taken to jumping Jim Crow, or jumping on Jim Crow, not on the stage

9

but in the courts, not in a dance but in lawsuits. With the Sipuel case in 1948 the courts began to oust him from postgraduate education and, before I had finished my study, had further advanced the cause with the Sweatt and McLaurin cases in 1950 and challenged segregation in elementary schools. The salience of civil rights in the 1948 campaign also made a strong impression on me.

Unlike Wharton, who at Millsaps College in Jackson, Mississippi, had been involved in interracial activities with nearby black colleges, I had no such experience until my postgraduate years in Chapel Hill, where I became active in an interracial chapter of the American Veterans Committee which, among other things, called for the admission of blacks to the university.

My dissertation topic was plainly relevant to live issues, for if race relations had once been suddenly changed by law in one direction, presumably they could be changed by law in another. Or, in the jargon of the time, there was evidence that stateways had changed folkways, rather quickly at that, a point forcefully illustrated by Pitchfork Ben Tillman himself. In 1895 on a train to Columbia, Tillman explained his plans for disfranchisement to a black reporter seated beside him, an act which three years later would have been a violation of state law.[11]

Clearly Wharton, too, better than a decade ahead of me, had worked out of a conviction that he was dealing with live issues. In his 1939 dissertation preface, in the very words which appeared in the 1947 book, he wrote that no serious person could believe that the modus vivendi (as he called it) worked out between 1865 and 1890 offered a final answer: "In fact, there is abundant evidence that it is even now breaking down, and that the rate of the breakdown is increasing." Against the odds, he expressed "reason to believe that these coming changes . . . will, to an extent at least, be intentional changes guided by the more intelligent and far-sighted leaders of both races. If this be true, it is

10

essential that more knowledge be gained of the forces that have been at work. . . . "[12]

By the time I had finished *South Carolina Negroes*, the forces at work had become far more evident, and my study quickly got into print in 1952, published by the University of South Carolina Press. One early and unforgettable compliment on the book came with a double edge. "You took a pretty liberal position in that book," said an older historian from South Carolina, "but you weren't offensive about it."

Two to three years after the book appeared, while I was at Louisiana State University, I set about drafting a proposal for a paper to be entitled "Wanted: A History of Racial Segregation." Somebody told me that he had seen a notice of some lectures by Vann Woodward on the subject. I wrote Woodward to inquire, and got in reply a set of page proofs for *The Strange Career of Jim Crow*.

There was more to the book than the attack on entrenched myths about Jim Crow, to be sure, but that was what caught the eye in the wake of the Brown case. I well remember the meeting of a Baton Rouge interracial group in the spring of 1956, at which with some gratification I heard an earnest young student explaining to the group that racial segregation had not always prevailed and citing examples drawn from my findings, which he in all probability had found quoted in *The Strange Career*.

To informed people today, of course, finding that race relations had a history is something like the hysterical discovery of the obvious. It did not seem so then. But the attention it got did bear out once again the truism that historians write out of a "frame of reference."

The discovery had an obvious relevance to the challenge then being mounted against the Plessy doctrine. If segregation was an institution of comparatively recent origin, and if laws and stateways had played a significant part in creating it, then laws and stateways might be used to alter or destroy it.

11

*George B. Tindall*

Around the mid-twentieth century segregation functioned as the most visible symbol of the modus vivendi. It not only became a prime target of attack; it also tended to affect the focus of historians. Yet few things grow dated as fast as yesterday's relevancy. I am still brought up short, for instance, by references to the "traditionally Democratic black vote."

On segregation, polls have shown sharp changes in white opinion. In 1942 only 2 percent of white children approached by the National Opinion Research Center said that white and black children should attend the same schools. By 1980, according to the Gallup Poll, only 5 percent of white Southern parents objected to sending a child to school with "a few" black children. Although the willingness weakened when they were asked about schools one-half or more black, it was nevertheless, as two writers called it, "one of the most complete turnarounds in the history of public opinion polling."[13]

Students nowadays seem to lack a grasp of the world of segregation. Racial antagonism and separatism they have witnessed. Forced segregation, separate waiting rooms, separate water fountains, they have not.

The civil rights movement proved ultimately to be a victim of its own success, but the movement gave a momentum to the study of black history that seems still far from having run its course. In an essay contributed to a *Festschrift* for Fletcher Green three decades ago, I suggested that the Age of Segregation had given rise to a peculiarly static image of black life.

At the end of that essay I cited Gunnar Myrdal's prognosis some twenty years before that the long "period of stagnation was only a temporary balancing of forces which was just on the verge of being broken." I added: "It does not require so bold a foresight to suggest that Negro historiography is only at the beginning of a similar release of forces. The next two decades will probably see an extensive historical invasion of areas . . . long forfeited to sociologists."[14] It was an easy call, I suppose, and events have borne it out.

But the victory of the civil rights movement had its limitations. Vernon Wharton, a far-sighted historian, wrote prophetically back in 1939: "Just as many vestigial remains of slavery are apparent in the present system, so may we expect many of the aspects of the present order to carry over into any system that may evolve out of it."[15] If the issues of today and tomorrow are likely to reach a focus on some symbolic issue, it seems likely that it will fall somewhere on the greatest vestigial remain of the postbellum modus vivendi—for that matter a remain of slavery: continuing economic bondage.

The civil rights movement, like Reconstruction, put the focus on legal rights; it did not put food on the table. Voting rights and desegregation were achieved, granted some glaring exceptions. Less was done about the context of dependency—poverty, unemployment, urban decay, slums, family—class issues which belong to a different order of complexity and which are not entirely the burden of one race.

NOTES

1. Dailey Paskman, "Gentlemen, Be Seated!" A Parade of the American Minstrels (New York: C. N. Potter, distributed by Crown, 1976), p. 9.

2. Robert C. Toll, Blacking Up: The Minstrel Show in Nineteenth Century America (New York: Oxford University Press, 1974), p. 28 and passim; Carl Wittke, Tambo and Bones: A History of the American Minstrel Stage (Durham, N.C.: Duke University Press, 1930), pp. 23–28, 31–35, and passim.

3. Toll, Blacking Up, pp. 30–31, 51–52.

4. Harriet Beecher Stowe, Uncle Tom's Cabin, or Life among the Lowly, The Library of America (New York: Literary Classics of the United States, distributed by Viking Press, 1982), p. 278.

5. Sir William A. Craigie and James R. Hulbert, A Dictionary of American English on Historical Principles (Chicago: University of Chicago Press,

George B. Tindall

1942), pp. 1343–44; Mitford M. Mathews, *A Dictionary of Americanisms on Historical Principles* (Chicago: University of Chicago Press, 1951), pp. 506–507.

6. Joseph Turpin Drake, "The Negro in Greenville, South Carolina," M.A. thesis, Department of Sociology, University of North Carolina, 1940, pp. 117–32.

7. George B. Tindall, *South Carolina Negroes, 1877–1900* (Columbia: University of South Carolina Press, 1952), p. 299.

8. Vernon Lane Wharton, *The Negro in Mississippi, 1865–1890*, The James Sprunt Studies in History and Political Science (Chapel Hill: University of North Carolina Press, 1947).

9. Alrutheus Ambush Taylor, *The Negro in South Carolina during the Reconstruction* (Washington, D.C.: Association for the Study of Negro Life and History, 1924).

10. E. Franklin Frazier, "The Booker T. Washington Papers," *The Library of Congress, Quarterly Journal of Current Acquisitions* 2 (February 1945): 24.

11. Tindall, *South Carolina Negroes*, p. 300.

12. Wharton, *The Negro in Mississippi*, pp. 5–6.

13. John Shelton Reed and Merle Black, "How Southerners Gave Up Jim Crow," *New Perspectives* (Fall 1985): 15–19.

14. George B. Tindall, "Southern Negroes since Reconstruction: Dissolving the Static Image," *Writing Southern History: Essays in Historiography in Honor of Fletcher M. Green*, ed. Arthur S. Link and Rembert W. Patrick (Baton Rouge: Louisiana State University Press, 1965), p. 361.

15. Wharton, *The Negro in Mississippi*, p. 6. In the dissertation the third word is "the." Wharton, "The Negro in Mississippi, 1865–1890," Ph.D. diss., Department of History, University of North Carolina, 1939, pp. 2–3.

Jumping Jim Crow

# 2. The Making of a Historian

Leon F. Litwack is Alexander F. and May T. Morrison Professor of American History at the University of California, Berkeley. He earned his B. A. in *1951*, his M. A. in *1952*, and his Ph.D. in *1958* at the University of California, Berkeley. He taught at the University of Wisconsin before returning to Berkeley in *1965* and has since taught as a Fulbright Professor of History at Moscow State, as a Ford Foundation Professor of Southern Studies at the University of Mississippi, as a lecturer in American history at the University of Helsinki, and as a Fulbright Lecturer in American History at the University of Sydney. He has held a Guggenheim Fellowship and a Rockefeller Foundation Fellowship and was elected to the American Academy of Arts and Sciences. He also served as president of the Organization of American Historians. His many publications include a widely used textbook on American history, North of Slavery: The Negro in the Free States, 1790–1860 *(1961)*, and Black Leaders of the Nineteenth Century *(1988)*, a collection of *essays edited with August Meier. His study of the emancipation experience,* Been in the Storm So Long: The Aftermath of Slavery *(1979)*, won the Francis Parkman Prize, the American Book Award in History, and the

*Pulitzer Prize in History. Professor Litwack continues to study race relations in post-Reconstruction America.*

Thirty-seven years ago, I came to New York for the first time, a graduate student at Berkeley gathering materials for a doctoral dissertation on free blacks in the antebellum North. My primary destination was 135th Street near Lenox Avenue in Harlem, a branch of the New York Public Library which housed the Schomburg Collection in African American history and culture. The library was all but empty. In the several months I spent there, I saw no one else using the manuscripts or rare books. It said something about the state of Negro history (as it was then called). No wonder a senior historian at Berkeley advised me, after I finished my Ph.D., that it was time to get back into the mainstream of American history. There were no positions in "Negro history," except at black colleges; no reputable history department recognized such a course—or the need for such a course.

What we define as "Negro" or "Afro-American" or "African American" history had its origins in the nineteenth century as an effort by black Americans to instill racial pride in their people and to justify emancipation and civil and political equality. In their pioneering work in the early twentieth century, Carter G. Woodson and W. E. B. Du Bois thought a scholarly study of the history of the black experience in the United States might help to undermine racism and raise the historical consciousness of both white and black Americans. But neither Woodson nor Du Bois merited much attention in a nation which embraced so passionately its racial and historical myths; neither historian, in fact, merited much attention from historians. That was consistent with a conception of history that excluded black people, that defined them out of American identity.

Historians and teachers of history did not simply reinforce prevailing racial and ethnic biases; they helped to create and shape them. They miseducated generations of Ameri-

*The Making of a Historian*

cans, including my generation. What dominated their perceptions of the past were the views of the exceptional, those in the political and economic elites who left the most substantial (in quantity) and the most easily accessible records, the kinds of records with which historians felt most comfortable. History was made by people who had the leisure to record their thoughts in journals, diaries, and letters. (Richard Hofstadter once said of Thomas Jefferson that the leisure that enabled him to write his treatises on human liberty was made possible by the labor of his several hundred slaves.) The history of ordinary people was thought to be impossible to recreate because traditional historical scholarship rested on records and documents which working class people, white and black, have not usually kept. The failure to bring to historical consciousness the experience of ordinary people was not a failure of the archives but of those who narrowly construed historical documentation; it was a breakdown of historical imagination.

My parents left no diaries, journals, or letters; they were not formally schooled, but they were articulate working-class people. They had come from Russia as youths, lived for a short time in the Jewish and Italian immigrant neighborhoods in New York, and hitchhiked out to California, ultimately to Santa Barbara, where I was born and raised. Although best known as an upper-middle-class haven, Santa Barbara did have a working class, people like my parents who serviced, in a variety of ways, the moneyed residents. My father was a gardener, my mother a seamstress, and we lived in a small rented house in a largely Mexican American neighborhood. Early on, my parents introduced me to a cultural world that helped to shape my thinking, reading, and listening, and they spoke often of those people they most admired, many of them well known (from Henry David Thoreau, Walt Whitman, and Leo Tolstoy to Franklin Delano Roosevelt and Mahatma Gandhi), many of them less known—rebels and dissidents (Eugene Debs, Big Bill Haywood, Emma Goldman) who had engaged themselves in

Leon F. Litwack

struggles for social justice. My neighborhood exposed me at the same time to a diversity of cultures, languages, histories, and experiences. I thought it a unique, exciting, often exhilarating education.

That education, however, often came into conflict with the uncritical celebration of America to which I was exposed in school and through the standard Hollywood fare, a sanitized, distorted version of reality that contradicted much of what I sensed, learned, and experienced outside the classroom. The history we were taught in school was largely the history of Anglo-Saxons and Northern Europeans. It was about Pilgrims, Puritans, and Founding Fathers. It was someone else's history, not my history, not the lives of my parents, friends, and neighbors. If Mexican Americans appeared at all in our textbooks, it was as exotic, picturesque appendages to a Europeanized mainstream. (Every year in Santa Barbara, we restaged history in the Spanish Fiesta; gaily costumed Kiwanis and Rotarians evoked, in the words of Carey McWilliams, "a past that never existed to cast some glamour on an equally unreal today.")

If African Americans were mentioned in my classes and textbooks, it was as docile and contented slaves or as easily manipulated and ignorant freedmen; their history was said to be a history of submission patiently and passively, even gladly endured. The textbook we read in high school was no more enlightened than the textbook used in most Ivy League colleges, in which Samuel Eliot Morison of Harvard and Henry Steele Commager of Columbia said of slavery, "Sambo suffered less than any other class in the South. Although brought here by force, the incurably optimistic negro soon became attached to the country and devoted to his 'white folks.' "

The textbook was my first confrontation with history. I asked my eleventh grade teacher for the opportunity to respond to the textbook's version of slavery and Reconstruction, to what I thought were distortions and racial biases.

*The Making of a Historian*

The research led me to the Public Library—and to W. E. B. Du Bois's *Black Reconstruction*, with its intriguing subtitle: "An Essay toward a History of the Part Which Black Folk Played in the Attempt to Reconstruct Democracy in America, 1860–1880." Armed with the findings of that book, I presented what I thought to be an absolutely persuasive rebuttal of the textbook. At the conclusion of my report, however, the teacher looked at the class and said, "Now students, you must remember that Leon is bitterly pro-labor." I failed to understand the relevance of her remark. Only some years later did I come to appreciate the thrust of her observation. My views of labor, my outspoken support of unions, my political and social activism had helped to shape—my teacher might have said prejudiced—my historical vision.

In my senior year, I edited the school newspaper, only to find myself embroiled in a running conflict with the vice principal, who several times threatened to shut us down over editorials and stories he deemed obscene or subversive. (We called for the removal of the *Reader's Digest* from English classes, we opposed compulsory military training and questioned the premises of the Cold War, and we thought the funds used each year to stage the Spanish Fiesta would be better spent on low-cost housing for Mexican Americans.) That same year, the National Conference of Christians and Jews honored our newspaper for its coverage of Brotherhood Week—a special issue in which we focused on the persistence and virulence of racism in American society.

When I came to Berkeley as an underclassman in 1948, political ferment was extensive and diverse, and my commitment to social activism flourished on a number of fronts, including opposition to those persistent and largely successful efforts to police and repress student political action and to certify the loyalty of faculty members. History, at the same time, continued to exert its fascination for me. Not one but several influences solidified my decision to teach and write American history: my activism (around such issues as loyalty oaths, racism, and the Cold War), my identifi-

Leon F. Litwack

cation with a trade union (the Marine Cooks and Stewards Union, which enabled me to "ship out" as a messman during summers and Christmas recess), and the many hours spent in the library stacks, nourishing my engagement with the past. Since high school, I had come to be moved by an awareness of the uses and abuses of the past and of the fundamental contradictions between my country's often proclaimed ideals and its practices, between its professed egalitarianism and deep inequalities in wealth and in conditions of work and life. Clearly, as my studies and observations had revealed, black Americans, more acutely than other Americans, had experienced the consequences of these contradictions. For them, in fact, the betrayal of expectations had been a way of life. (My senior thesis exposed still another troubling historical fact: the hostility of the American labor movement to black workers.)

A chance meeting in my junior year at Berkeley proved memorable. A friend (a graduate student in history) called and asked me to come over to his apartment; he said someone wanted to meet me. I was ushered into the living room, and I recognized his guest immediately—it was W. E. B. Du Bois. Of course I was deeply impressed; I had read his books. But why had he singled me out? He wanted, he said, to meet an undergraduate in history. He wanted to know what I was learning about slavery and Reconstruction. My response was in two parts: the textbook (by John D. Hicks) reflected familiar distortions and biases; the course lectures did not, and their content impressed and astonished Du Bois, as they revealed new ways of thinking about both slavery and Reconstruction. The person teaching the course was a young assistant professor, Kenneth M. Stampp, who would have a profound impact on my thinking and with whom I would ultimately write my dissertation.

My political and social commitments had no doubt influenced the way I looked at history, but history had also helped to inform and shape my political and social commitments. Most of all, I wanted my work as a historian and

The Making of a Historian

a teacher to make a difference. History was more than the dead past; the way in which it was written and taught had consequences, and black Americans, in particular, had seen how it might be used both to explain and sustain their repression. The traditional view of Reconstruction, for example, retained a profound impact on race relations. The way in which the history of that unique experiment in biracial democratic government came to be written and believed, the way in which it came to be portrayed on the screen for nearly a century in such popular classics as *Birth of a Nation* and *Gone with the Wind*, helped to justify a complex of racial laws, practices, and beliefs—most of all, the inferior position assigned to black men and women, politically, socially, and economically.

My first book, *North of Slavery: The Negro in the Free States, 1790–1860*, appeared in 1961, seven years after the Supreme Court outlawed segregated education. Massive, often violent resistance had thwarted the initial efforts to implement the Court's decision. *North of Slavery* examined the degree to which white racial attitudes in America transcended regional boundaries, including the Mason-Dixon line. Although free, blacks in the North remained an anomaly, largely disfranchised, segregated, and economically oppressed. Discrimination barred them from the election polls, juries, schools, and workshops, as well as from many libraries, theaters, lecture halls, and public conveyances. And having excluded blacks from such facilities, whites turned the exclusion against blacks: that is, having deprived blacks of opportunities for economic, cultural, and political advancement, whites scorned blacks for their poverty; ignorance; lack of culture, refinement, and civic virtue, and confidently declared them incapable of improvement.

Published in 1961, the book was warmly received in unanticipated places—in the white Southern press, not necessarily in the book review section but on the editorial page. Several editors embraced this indictment of Northern racial hypocrisy, using the book to remind their readers that the

Leon F. Litwack

"Negro problem" was deeply rooted and that racial bigotry was not the unique property of the South. "Race Prejudice Had Origins in North," said a Miami newspaper. The *Memphis Commercial* entitled its review, "Jim Crow Bar Not Regional." The reviewer in the *Raleigh News & Observer* concluded, "Since Northern whites were so adamant against the Negro a century ago, they should show more sympathy & understanding toward the slow change in contemporary Southern attitudes."

I left Berkeley in 1958 to teach at the University of Wisconsin. When I returned to the University of California six years later, the harmonious political, intellectual, and social system characteristic of the past several decades was coming apart, and the legitimacy of our institutions, our dominant values, and our assumptions was being disputed as never before. Historians, like others, would be very much affected by the civil rights movement, the domestic and campus upheavals, and the war in Vietnam. Growing numbers of scholars, white and black, began to turn their attention to groups long excluded from historical study, to people who had spent their lives in relative obscurity, who had never shared the fruits of affluence, who had never enjoyed power—the very people who had initially inspired my interest in history. In seeking to capture their historical experience, both in my books and in the classroom, I now found myself with plenty of company. The Schomburg Library, upon my return there in the mid-1960s, was bulging with researchers, and the ongoing scholarship in African American history was forcing historians to reassess all of American history. For two centuries, if not longer, black Americans by their very presence had tested the quality of America's commitment to its professed principles. That unique position had afforded black men and women a very different perspective on this country and some of its most revered traditions and institutions. That perspective was now being accorded the scrutiny and respect it had long deserved.

The study of American history would never be the same

*The Making of a Historian*

again. The kind of history being written and taught, the introduction of new perspectives and cultural experiences, reflected to a degree the changing makeup of the profession—much to the consternation of one eminent senior historian, who in his presidential address to the American Historical Association in 1962 voiced the fear that increasingly American history was being written by "products of lower middle class or foreign origins," "in a very real sense outsiders on our past," whose "emotions not infrequently get in the way of historical reconstructions," and who are incapable of understanding and communicating the historical products of other cultural environments. (Ironically, this was the same senior historian who some years earlier had advised me to get back into the mainstream of American history.)

When Fisk University in 1929 recorded the experiences of former slaves, one of the interviewees asked the interviewer, "In all the books you never have studied Negro history, have you? If you want Negro history you'll have to get it from somebody who wore the shoe, and by and by from one to the other, you will get a book." That admonition pervaded much of the new work in African American history, and it helped to shape my study of the aftermath of slavery. North of Slavery had focused on white racial attitudes. Been in the Storm So Long, as its title (a nineteenth-century black spiritual) suggested, reflected a different spirit and strikingly different sources. I asked some simple questions of the materials, but the answers were filled with unexpected complexity and ambiguity and, not unexpectedly, with extraordinary drama: What happens to an enslaved people when they are freed? How free was free? To what could a freed black man or woman aspire in a society where whites owned the land, the tools, the crops, and the law, and where the prospect of black freedom made it all the more imperative that they retain control? To capture the profound drama of emancipation, that moment when a people who had never known anything but slavery encountered the exhilaration, the terror, and the uncertainties of

Leon F. Litwack

freedom, it was essential to recover the black voice, to record how newly freed black men and women perceived and acted on their freedom.

This was the chance to examine slavery at the moment it came apart, when whites and blacks confronted each other in new and unprecedented ways. What the Civil War did was to sweep away the pretenses, dissolve the illusions, and lay bare the tensions and instability inherent in the master-slave relationship. For slaveholding families, the Civil War came to be a moment of truth. The War taught the master who claimed to "know" the Negro best that he knew the Negro least of all, that he had mistaken the outward demeanor of his slaves for their inner feelings, the docility of his slaves for contentment, the deference and obedience of his slaves for submission.

Some thirty years after *North of Slavery*, I have turned from the Jim Crow North to the Jim Crow South, to the first generation of black Southerners born in freedom and the character and the mechanisms of their response to the society they entered. The study focuses on how this generation came to be initiated into the racial rites and mores of the "redeemed" South (their "baptism of racial emotion," as Richard Wright called it), how they were instructed in the arts of survival and accommodation, how they learned to wear the mask in the presence of whites (Ralph Ellison once called Southern life the most dramatic form of life in the United States, because it was so full of actors, white and black), and the patterns of thought and behavior that set this generation off from their slave-born parents and kin, particularly in the relations and demeanor they sustained with whites.

To examine this generation is to appreciate the continuing white obsession with racial security, the spectacular increase in the frequency, sadism, and exhibitionism of racial violence, the felt need to disfranchise and segregate a people perceived as an increasing source of social danger, subversion, and contamination. It is to tell the story, too, of young

*The Making of a Historian*

black men and women seeking to shed the remaining vestiges of slavery, testing in new ways the limits of permissible dissent, opting in many cases to reject the norms and values of conventional society. What whites perceived in the 1890s was a generation that largely complied with the racial order, but not with the same agreeableness, the same bodily and facial movements, the requisite grin. No wonder the white South felt compelled to monitor this generation with increased vigilance.

The operation of the racial system in the lives of black Southerners—the gratuitous insults and humiliations, the Jim Crow signs that screamed at them from every direction, disfranchisement, the educational limitations (that is, enforced ignorance), the impediments to landownership, the hopelessly compromised and corrupted legal system, the lynch mobs—rested on the compelling need to remind blacks of their place, that color marked them as inferior in the eyes of whites, no matter how they conducted themselves, no matter how diligently they performed their duties, no matter what might be their social class or educational or economic attainments. For black Southerners, there was never a purely economic way out of their difficulties: a fact white Populists in the late nineteenth century, like many white radicals, black leaders, and black editors in the twentieth century, failed to understand—or preferred to ignore.

It is in many ways a dreary story. To accommodate or to resist. Who can presume to know now what those blacks who lived at the time were prepared to suffer in the name of one strategy or another. But even as black men and women made their peace with the ruling race, even as they learned to accommodate and mask their feelings in the presence of whites, many found ways to impart meaning to their lives. If most were forced to accommodate, they did not necessarily submit. There were limits, and where and how black Southerners chose to impose those limits is very much a part of their history—and American history.

Leon F. Litwack

To appreciate the quality, the depth, the resiliency, the extraordinary variety and resourcefulness of the black response to their "place" in the South, we need, as historians, to reassess the traditional ways we choose to document the past, to be sensitive to the diverse, usually nonpolitical ways in which a people conveyed their thoughts and feelings about matters of daily and far-reaching concern to them, often in a language deliberately incomprehensible to whites. It is, as Lawrence Levine has suggested, to enter a world in which the spoken, chanted, sung, or shouted word often became the primary form of communication. In documenting the black South, I have learned as much from novelists, poets, musicians, photographers, and artists as I have from academic historians; they have illuminated the past for me in ways that are difficult if not impossible for a mere historian to capture. And for the study of African American history, they have been especially invaluable: the poetry of a Sterling Brown and a Langston Hughes, the prose of a Jean Toomer, a Zora Neale Hurston, a Ralph Ellison, a Richard Wright, or a Toni Morrison, the photographs of a P. J. Polk, a James VanDerZee, or a Richard Samuel Roberts, the artistry of an Aaron Douglass, a Jacob Lawrence, or a Romaire Bearden.

And, as critical as any of these artists, there is the eloquent matter-of-factness conveyed by the bluesmen and blueswomen. It has been suggested that some of the most spirited, some of the bleakest and most anguished nonfiction in the American idiom may be found in their work, in the toughness, the tensions, the passion, the wisdom and wit, the immediacy of a Charley Patton, a Robert Johnson, a Son House, a Tommy Johnson, a Ma Rainey, a Muddy Waters. Curiously, these names are absent from the dictionaries of American and African American biography. Nor may one find their lyrics in literary anthologies. But to listen to them is to feel more vividly, more intensely than any mere poet, novelist, or historian could convey, the thoughts, passions,

The Making of a Historian

and frightening honesty of a new generation of black Southerners. "How much thought can be hidden in a few short
lines of poetry," asks Robert Palmer in his book *Deep Blues*.
"How much history can be transmitted by pressure on a
guitar string?" And he answers, "The thought of generations, the history of every human being who's ever felt the
blues come down like showers of rain."

One can hear it in Willie Brown's plaintive lament, as he
despairs of effecting any changes in his life or prospects:

> Can't tell my future, I can't tell my past.
> Lord, it seems like every minute sure gon' be my last.
> Oh, a minute seems like hours, and hours seems like days.
> And a minute seems like hours, hour seems like days;

or in the chilling fantasy described by Furry Lewis, born in
1900, raised in the Delta:

> I believe I'll buy me a graveyard of my own,
> I believe I'll buy me a graveyard of my own,
> I'm goin' kill everybody that have done me wrong;

or in the bluesy dirge sounded by Charley Patton, born near
Edwards, Mississippi, in the early 1880s:

> Ev'ry day, seems like murder here
> Ev'ry day, seems like murder here
> I'm gonna leave tomorrow, I know you don't want me here;

or in the profound insights offered by this bluesman:

> Well, I drink to keep from worrying and I laugh to keep from
>    crying,
> Well, I drink to keep from worrying and I laugh to keep from
>    crying,
> I keep a smile on my face so the public won't know my mind.
>
> Some people thinks I am happy but they sho' don't know my
>    mind,
> Some people thinks I am happy but they sho' don't know my
>    mind,

Leon F. Litwack

> They see this smile on my face, but my heart is bleeding all
> the time.

And how much history may be imparted in but two lines, in the desperation voiced by blueswoman Bertha "Chippie" Hill:

> I'm gonna lay my head on a lonesome railroad line
> And let the 219 pacify my mind.

To explore on one level the history of African Americans is to find incredible atrocities and repression. It is easy enough to be shaken by the documentation, to bemoan the extraordinary waste of human potential—the generations denied the opportunity to make something of their lives. Perhaps the real story, however, is not the story of victims but of survivors, how so many individuals and families managed to transcend their condition, how they established communities and kept families together. Ralph Ellison once suggested that any people who could endure so much brutalization and keep together and endure "is obviously more than the sum of its brutalization. Seen in this perspective, theirs has been one of the great human experiences and one of the great triumphs of the human spirit in modern times."

The study of race relations, however, has not left me optimistic about the eradication of racism in American society. What the civil rights movement achieved was impressive, far reaching in the ways it changed the face of the South—if not the nation. But it was revealing, too, for the paradoxes and contradictions it exposed. For all the political gains, the dismantling of Jim Crow, the mass marches, the optimistic rhetoric, many of the same tensions and anxieties persisted and festered. Even as the civil rights movement struck down legal barriers, it failed to dismantle economic barriers. Even as it ended the violence of segregation, it failed to diminish the violence of poverty. Even as it ended school segregation by law, it failed to end segregation by income and tradition. Even as it transformed the face of Southern politics,

*The Making of a Historian*

it did nothing to reallocate resources, to redistribute wealth and income. Even as it entered schools and colleges, voting booths and lunch counters, it failed to penetrate the corporate boardrooms and federal bureaucracies where the most critical decisions affecting American lives were made. Even as it increased the black middle class, it left behind a greater number of black Americans to endure lives of quiet despair and hopelessness.

Some 130 years after emancipation, some three decades after the civil rights revolution, American society finds itself in an ongoing, a heightened racial crisis. The brutalizing effects of more than two centuries of slavery and another century of enforced segregation and miseducation continue to shape race relations, continue to hold up a mirror to Americans, to test the democratic experiment, the principles and values Americans embrace. Racism remains the most debilitating virus in the American system, nourished by historical and cultural illiteracy. More than twenty years have passed since the Kerner Commission warned that the United States was "moving toward two societies, one black, one white— separate and unequal." That process continues, often with more subtlety and not nearly as capable of provoking the moral outrage that helped sustain the civil rights movement. But no matter how it is measured—by where most blacks live, their income, the schools they attend, or their future prospects—this nation remains in critical ways two societies, separate and unequal, racism remains deeply embedded in our culture, and the consequences spill over into almost every facet of American life. The victims threaten to become, if tens of thousands have not already become, a large shadow population of interior exiles, aliens in their own land, locked into a cycle of deprivation and despair, empty of belief or hope, and highly volatile.

Whatever the substantial advances made since World War II, there remains the forcefulness of a warning sounded by W. E. B. Du Bois in the 1930s: that what black Americans face is not simply the rational, the conscious determination

Leon F. Litwack

of whites to oppress them but "age long complexes sunk now largely to unconscious habit and irrational urge." When some 50 percent of black children grow up in poverty, when infant mortality rates in the inner cities surpass those in Third World countries, when the life expectancy of whites and blacks widens to historic dimensions, when functional illiteracy and joblessness loom as likely possibilities for black youths, when public schools deteriorate in the wake of white flight and neglect, this nation finds itself locked in a war at home, where men and women confront dangers and conditions that often exceed those faced in more conventional conflicts. The enemies in this war are poverty, homelessness, unemployment, racism, sickness, and disease—problems not susceptible to surgical strikes, carpet bombings, smart missiles, or macho posturing.

I still think about that day in high school when I hoped (with all my youthful idealism and enthusiasm) to change the way my classmates and teacher thought about race, slavery, and Reconstruction. Some forty-five years later, I would like to think my work has made some difference—the publications, the lectures, the films and film consultations, but perhaps most importantly my teaching, the nearly 30,000 students I have taught at Berkeley over the past thirty years, mostly in the survey American history course (which I continue to teach), and in the course on the History of African Americans and Race Relations, and the students I have had the privilege to teach as a visitor at Moscow State University, Beijing University, the University of Sydney, the University of South Carolina, Louisiana State University, and the University of Mississippi.

Teaching remains for me a critical challenge: to force students to see and feel the past in ways that may be genuinely disturbing, to reexamine their assumptions, to test, sometimes to undermine old dogmas and values; to enable them to overcome racial stereotypes and cultural parochialism, to understand the deep historical roots of racism, and to ap-

*The Making of a Historian*

preciate the formidable barriers this nation erected against black advancement. And it is that rare opportunity to raise to the surface of history the men and women, the known and the unknown, many of them losers in their own time, outlaws, rebels who—individually or collectively—tried to flesh out, to give meaning to abstract notions of liberty, equality, and freedom, who demonstrated, marched, agitated, went to prison, sometimes gave their lives to question the assumptions and wisdom of those who held power.

As I look out on each assemblage of students I have addressed, both in this country and abroad, I have expressed the hope that they will produce their share of dissidents, rebels, and disturbers of the peace, men and women who will choose to question our sanity and values, the aimless violence and materialist obsessions, the hypocrisies, absurdities, and contradictions, a new generation for whom personal commitment to social and racial justice will be nothing less than a moral imperative, and who will opt for the highest kind of loyalty to their country—a willingness to unmask its leaders and subject its institutions and ideology to critical examination. History teaches us that it is not the rebels, it is not the curious, it is not the dissidents who endanger a society but rather the accepting, the unthinking, the unquestioning, the docile, the obedient, the silent, and the indifferent. This lesson, as I have tried to convey to my students, not only in Berkeley but in Moscow, Beijing, and Oxford, Mississippi, knows no state or national boundaries. And it remains timeless.

"The problem of the 20th century is the problem of the color line," W. E. B. Du Bois wrote in 1903 in *The Souls of Black Folk*, "the relation of the darker to the lighter races of men in Asia and Africa, in America and the islands of the sea." Half a century later, Du Bois added a dimension to that problem: "Today I see more clearly than yesterday that back of the problem of race and color, lies a greater problem which both obscures and implements it: and that is the fact that so many civilized persons are willing to live in comfort

Leon F. Litwack

even if the price of this is poverty, ignorance and disease of the majority of their fellow men." That judgment is even more poignant today. And its consequences remain as far reaching and devastating. The problem of the twenty-first century will remain in large part the color line, but it will be fought out and resolved in a very different America (an America one-third black and Hispanic) and in a strikingly different world, a world in which the great majority of people are nonwhite, many of them with long memories, many of them with a vivid sense of history.

From the Mississippi Delta, in the early twentieth century, bluesman Robert Johnson articulated a lonely and terrifying sense of personal betrayal and anguish that transcended both time and region. He suggested a society impossible to overcome—or to escape. There was no way to assimilate. There was no way to separate:

> I got to keep moving, I got to keep moving
> blues falling down like hail
> blues falling down like hail
> Uumh, blues falling down like hail
> blues falling down like hail
> and the days keeps on 'minding me
> there's a hellhound on my trail,
> hellhound on my trail.

*The Making of a Historian*

# 3. Reflections of a Reconstructed White Southerner

Dan T. Carter is William Rand Kenan, Jr., Professor of History at Emory University in Atlanta, Georgia. He earned his B.A. at the University of South Carolina in *1962*, his M.A. at the University of Wisconsin in *1964*, and his Ph.D. at the University of North Carolina at Chapel Hill in *1967*, where he studied with George B. Tindall. He also taught at the University of Maryland and the University of Wisconsin before becoming Andrew Mellon Professor in the Humanities at Emory in *1974*. He is a past president of the Southern Historical Association and during the *1995–96* academic year served as Pitt Professor at Cambridge University. His first book, Scottsboro: A Tragedy of the American South (*1969*), won numerous awards, including the Bancroft Prize in History. When the War Was Over: The Failure of Self-Reconstruction in the South, 1865–1867 (*1985*), his second book, also won acclaim, earning the Organization of American Historians' *Avery Craven Award*. His many honors include a fellowship at the National Humanities Center. Professor Carter is also the author of George Wallace, Richard Nixon, and the Transformation of American Politics (*1992*), *which he had presented as the Charles Edmondson Historical Lectures at Baylor University. He recently published* The Politics of Rage: George Wallace, the Origins of the New Conservatism, and the Transformation of American Politics, *which won the Robert F. Kennedy Book Award. Most recently he published* From George Wallace to Newt Gingrich: Race in the Conservative Counterrevolution, 1963–1994, *which was originally delivered as the Walter Lynwood Fleming Lectures in Southern History at Louisiana State University. Professor Carter continues to study the South in American history.*

When I received Professor Cimbala's letter asking me to write a paper reflecting upon the ways in which my life has shaped my work as a historian, I was initially at a loss for a response. I am not sure I have ever thought about the books and articles I have written as representing a "body of work." Like a carpenter—which I was for several summers—I simply set myself to the task of building the next split-level or remodeling another kitchen. If there are connections, I suppose they are linked by my belief that the search for moral justice should lie at the heart of our civic culture. This does not mean that I embrace the notion that "history" is simply a weapon to be used as a tool in a struggle for ideological dominance. I remain committed to the importance of careful historical research and documentation as well as balance and fairness. But the mainspring of my concerns remains the story of that search for moral justice.

That I acknowledge. Still I remain uneasy at the prospect of drawing a link between that work and the story of my own life. Questions about those connections are perfectly legitimate, but they seem to suggest a kind of 1990s version of scholarly analysis through self-therapy. I began to have visions of an academic Iron John movement—the West

*Reflections of a Reconstructed White Southerner*

Coast self-help therapy that has tried to help men by having them go out in the woods, beat some drums, stand around in a circle, and get in touch with their feelings. As fellow Southerner Charles Reagan Wilson has observed, however, when white Southern men stand around in a circle and get in touch with their feelings, something terrible is likely to happen.

I'm also conscious of the pitfalls that lie in relying upon memories of my past. Much of my recent research on a study of George Wallace and American politics in the 1960s and 1970s has involved oral interviews, about 150 hours altogether. I have talked to dozens of individuals, asking them to relive their experiences in the 1950s, 60s, and 70s. I have found their stories sometimes humorous, sometimes moving, and always revealing. But I have also immersed myself in the more contemporary sources of the past. As I have listened to my interviewees describe the events of those years, I have recognized the great chasm between their recollections and what I know to be true. And with each interview, I have learned an important lesson about memory. It is not simply that we forget; the more fundamental problem is that we constantly recreate memory so that our past can live comfortably with the present without the jarring dissonances which inevitably accompany change through time. Like Shakespeare's monster, Caliban, we drift into reveries of a past that is so beautiful that when we wake we cry to dream again. And our dreams become our memories.

Still, if I am to recreate the links between my own past and the work I have chosen as a scholar, I have no choice but to tug at the threads of that past through recollection.

I was born in rural eastern South Carolina on a tobacco farm in the early summer of 1940. Although the community where I grew up was less than a hundred miles from the seventeenth-century city of Charleston, it remained a wilderness until the nineteenth century. The "Pee Dee" is

Dan T. Carter

the name given to the region from the river of the same name. It is an area of sandy soil and mixed pine and hardwood stands punctuated by creeks and swamps. Only with the spread of the cotton culture in the 1820s was much of the land cleared. Toward the end of the century, the introduction of light, flue-cured "cigarette" tobacco brought a second agricultural transformation and a modest economic upturn. Still it remained a relatively poor agricultural region.

My family on both sides drifted down from eastern North Carolina and settled in the region in the 1760s. Over the next one hundred and fifty years, they moved through cycles of relative affluence and poverty. Great-great-grandfather Giles Carter was a landowner of considerable wealth who accumulated several thousand acres and more than 100 slaves by the 1840s, but that wealth slipped away during the war and in the years that followed. By the time I was born at the tail end of the Depression, my father had spent the first thirty years of his life struggling to save a farm—the old homeplace we called it—which had been a part of our family for generations. As a small child, we still drank from a hand pump on the back porch. In my earliest and haziest memories I can even recall the privy that sat out behind the house. From the time I was six, I had a long list of chores around the farm. By my ninth year I was working in the tobacco fields, from dawn to dusk during harvest season. The building where I went to grade school—two grades to the class—would be condemned in many third world countries; my high school was a ramshackle frame building heated by pot-bellied coal stoves stoked each morning in a rotation shared by one of the eighteen members of my graduating class.

Lest I raise for you the echoes of a barefoot past straight out of Erskine Caldwell's *Tobacco Road*, I should confess that my mother was an honors college graduate who had taught Latin and whose mastery of the rules of English grammar still shames me by example. My father farmed, but by the

*Reflections of a Reconstructed White Southerner*

time I was six or seven he had begun to earn a comfortable living as a small building contractor. Both encouraged me to read, to think independently, and to dream of a world beyond the close-knit community that had been the home of the Carters and the Lawhons for more than 150 years. If my family seems deprived, it is only by today's standards. In the impoverished rural world of my childhood, we were comfortably middle class. I worked long hours in the fields not because of economic necessity but because my father believed that manual labor—particularly grueling manual labor in the fields—created inner reserves of fortitude and self-discipline even as they taught essential lessons about the dignity of labor.

The universe in which I lived as a child and a teenager was of course the world of the segregated South. I use the term segregated with some sense of the irony of the word. It was an oppressive culture in which blacks were relegated to the bottom rung of every economic ladder and barred by law from the schools of my childhood, by custom from the ballot box of my community. But it was hardly segregated. My earliest playmates were black. From the summer I was nine, I worked ten-hour days, five days a week in the fields, side by side with black men and women.

And each year, at the end of the summer's long tobacco harvest season, at least two of the landlords for whom we had worked would stage a "last cropping" dinner. With the tobacco cropped, strung, and securely hung in the barns, we would go over to the pump and freshen up while the landowner and his wife spread out the meal. There would be fish stew, a unique eastern Carolina dish, a spicy mixture of freshwater bream and redbreast cooked in a rich tomato sauce and poured over rice—all washed down with sweet iced tea and loaf after loaf of soft, sliced bread. I can still smell the wood fires under the black pots of stew and the pungent sweetness of the tobacco barns, saturated from generations of curing tobacco with oak wood fires. As I sat with the other children, teenagers, and womenfolk and fin-

Dan T. Carter

ished off the evening with a plate of fresh hand-churned ice cream, I would watch the men as they drifted away out under the trees and began passing mason jars of corn whiskey, laughing nervously like little boys away from the censoring eyes of womenfolks and respectability.

I saw nothing incongruous about the promiscuous mixing of black and white or the absurdity of those nuanced cultural conventions which decreed that—since the sky was overhead—it was permissible to eat side by side in a way that would have triggered a riot in one of the handful of restaurants in nearby Florence. And when I saw the two mason jars of corn whiskey passed around, one for blacks and one for whites, I saw, but I did not see.

Still, there were moments of disquiet, even unease. For a rural child of the 1940s and the 1950s, few events were more eagerly awaited than the annual County Fair. Since I raised cattle and showed them in the livestock exhibition it meant essentially a week away from school, often sleeping in the barns and slipping away during the afternoons for walks through the carnival booths and rides. At ten or eleven, as a pre-pubescent boy, the highlight of these excursions on the sawdust-covered midway was to slip to the edge of the crowd facing one of the two burlesque tents in which a dozen skimpily clad girls paraded to the entreaties of the barker who promised those who paid their 50 cents ("Men only over the age of 18") a far more revealing look inside the tent. I say two burlesque shows, because one was white and the other was black, or "colored," as it was called.

The week afterward, I spent a Saturday afternoon fishing on Lynch's creek with my cousin and two young black teenagers. They were a little older than me; one would say they were "boys" like myself except for the painful twist of meaning that word has come to have for black men. All of us, it turns out, had been to the fair. It did not occur to me that it was peculiar that there was a single "colored day" set

*Reflections of a Reconstructed White Southerner*

aside for my black friends. That too was simply part of the world in which we lived. I began talking about how beautiful I had thought the "colored girls" were at the fair. I certainly did not mean my comments in a predatory way; I thought of it as a compliment. I, as a white boy, was generously recognizing the beauty of an inferior race. I do not remember what my black friends said, but I distinctly remember that both recoiled as though they had been physically struck. One stood and simply walked away without saying a word.

Afterward, still bewildered, I told the story to my mother. She groped for some way to try and help me understand the taboos I had unknowingly violated. Finally, she said: "What if they had started talking about how beautiful the white girls were at the fair?"

I listened, but I still did not understand.

But then my world—the world of the white South— turned upside down one morning in the spring of 1954. Mr. M. L. Anderson, the principal of the little school I attended, called together the seventh through twelfth graders in the rickety auditorium to announce that the Supreme Court of the United States had passed a decision outlawing the separation of the races in the schools. We were likely to encounter "colored friends" or acquaintances who might be boastful or taunting, he warned, and we must respond with restraint as young ladies and gentlemen, implicitly young white ladies and gentlemen.

But there were no taunts, only silence as a wall of fear and anger divided black from white. And as the first halting challenges to the racial status quo emerged, I became a part of the white South as it mobilized for massive resistance. It is difficult to recreate the memories of those special pleasures of oppression. What did they know of us? Why did they taunt and abuse us? Our "colored" people were happy and contented; it was those hated Yankees, those outside agitators who were creating turmoil and conflict where only

Dan T. Carter

peace had prevailed. Why did they seek to turn our tranquil lives upside down? By us, of course, I meant "us" in a tribal sense—the white South.

While the battles to maintain the Southern way of life—my way of life—were fought in distant places—Montgomery, Alabama, Clinton, Tennessee, and Little Rock, Arkansas—there were closer skirmishes as well. In the nearby town of Florence, a local white policeman known sardonically by the black community as "Mr. Thug" badly beat a black man after he had—in the words of the officer—"sassed me." When a group of angry young black men smashed several windows in the downtown block-long black shopping district, club-wielding city police and the sheriff's department mobilized a show of force that would have done justice to one of the great urban riots of the next decade. Like most whites, I thrilled to the mobilization of white resistance. After nearly three years of passivity in the face of growing black "impudence," it was a chance to strike back.

Several weeks after the mini-riot, my cousin James was home for the Christmas holidays, visiting from his home north of Miami. James was eighteen years older than me. My parents had taken him in during his teenage years after his father kicked him out of the house at age fifteen. In 1942 he left our rural community and enlisted in the Seabees, the Navy's construction and engineering arm. At Tarawa and later on Iwo Jima he worked round the clock constructing runways, several times under Japanese sniper fire. In the 1940s he was a war hero; in the 1950s he became—to me at least—a romantic adventurer as he moved to Florida, bought a 120-foot schooner, and sailed the Caribbean carrying supplies to remote islands. I worshipped him with the kind of intensity most youngsters today seem to reserve for sports heroes or rap stars.

As I described with some enthusiasm, I am sad to say, the way in which local police had showed those "niggers"—and that is the word I used—who was in charge, James stopped my account in mid-sentence. During the war, he told me, Navy units were generally segregated in the Pacific. But under the desperate pressure to throw up airstrips and emergency housing, the black and white labor battalions of the Seabees were soon working side by side. In late 1944, said James, he became desperately ill with fever and dysentery and was sent off to an understaffed field hospital where he thought he was going to die, where he wished, he said, he could die.

But for the next week, every spare moment they had, two of his black friends took turns sitting with him, helping him to the latrine, feeding him, cleaning him when he fouled himself, nursing him back to health. In many ways, I suppose it was a cliched story straight out of a Hollywood script: white sailor, saved by black friend, abandons racism. However banal, for him it was real. "When I got better," he said as he looked intently at me, "I swore I would never again use that word that way. I grew up hearing it day and night: the 'niggers' did this, the 'niggers' did that. Someday you'll understand. It's a kind of sickness. And people think the only cure is to find somebody to hate."

I wish I could say that this gentle rebuke was an epiphany; that, like Paul on the road to Damascus, the scales dropped away from my eyes. But that was not the case. I was simply embarrassed and hurt at the shaming administered by someone I loved. But I like to think—at least in retrospect—that my cousin had planted a time bomb which ticked away silently over the next three years.

If so, the change for me came completely in four intense years between 1958 and 1962. During those first two years I attended night classes at a local community college while I worked as a reporter at the *Florence Morning News*. Much of the work was the usual regimen of a rookie reporter: writing obituaries, covering the local tobacco warehousemen's convention and the latest multiple-car accident. But on the eve of my employment at the *News*, local Klansmen had just driven the editor of the *News* out of town for daring to argue

Dan T. Carter

that *Brown v. Board of Education* was the law of the land. And even though Jack O'Dowd's successor, James Rogers, was more cautious in his editorial policies, he and most of the older reporters with whom I worked made no effort to conceal their disdain for the old order of white supremacy. By the time I stood in a noisy Kress five-and-ten-cent store in the spring of 1960 and watched raucous whites screaming obscenities at the dozen well-dressed young black men and women sitting quietly at the lunch counter, I realized that the racial moorings of a lifetime had been severed.

My next two years at the University of South Carolina completed that transformation. Only in the years that followed did I realize how blessed I had been by the chance to meet and work with an extraordinary group of men and women. Many memories of my childhood are gone; I honestly cannot recall the name of a single university classmate who was not involved with me in the civil rights movement. But I do remember those people who became my friends for life: James McBride Dabbs, the Maysville, South Carolina, planter turned author and civil rights leader; John Lewis, the Student Nonviolent Coordinating Committee (SNCC) organizer and founder whom I first met at a civil rights retreat in Highlander, Tennessee; the Reverend Will Campbell, Connie Curry, and a dozen others. And there were my three roommates: Hayes Mizell, who went on to become a field organizer for the American Friends Service Committee's Southern project and a life-long activist for human rights; Charles Joyner, who went on to capture the memory of a low-country slave community in his eloquent book, *Down by the Riverside*; and fellow historian Selden Smith, whose good humor reminded me that commitment need not become self-righteousness. Most of all, I have kept with me the memory of those women who had struggled so hard to keep alive the dream of racial justice during the height of racial reaction in the 1950s and early 1960s: Alice Spearman, the head of the South Carolina Council on Human Relations; Libby Ledeen of the university's YWCA; and Mae Gautier, a young university Methodist chaplain. By the time I entered graduate school at the University of Wisconsin in the fall of 1962, I was committed to thinking and writing about the history of my region and its tortured relationship with the rest of the nation.

The few letters I wrote during this period that remain are almost painful in their naivete and idealism. Rebirth for white Southerners was painful, but all the sweeter for the liberation it brought. Like obdurate sinners who had suddenly been redeemed by grace, I confidently looked forward to a day when the beloved community that we knew in the civil rights movement would become a reality for the nation.

I believed that was possible because I knew that nestled side by side with the racial cruelties of my childhood were memories of a loving world of kinfolk, neighbors, and friends; a world governed by obligations and responsibilities to family, church, and neighbors. In that world, even the harshest edges of racial hatred could be softened by the daily human exchanges of the rural South. I can still remember working as a poll worker at my local community in the summer Democratic primary of 1962. Over the previous two years the number of black registered voters in that rural precinct had gone from less than a half dozen to more than 100. As we set up the tables and ballot box and stacked the blank ballots, my uncle—who was in charge of the voting—groused about all the "Kennedy-loving" blacks who would be casting their ballots.

But when those black voters came to pick up their blank ballots, he greeted them with a smile, a joke, and a solicitous question about their children or the state of their tobacco crop. Afterward, as we counted the ballots, I teased him a bit and it was his turn to be embarrassed. "Well, most of 'em are neighbors," he said apologetically.

In some ways that mixture of indignation and hope was

Dan T. Carter

the background to my career as a historian. My dissertation and my first book, *Scottsboro: A Tragedy of the American South*, was an initial attempt to find my own voice as a historian. In it, I tried to tell the story of one of the great civil rights cases of the twentieth century. The case began in the early spring of 1931, when Alabama authorities arrested nine black teenagers in the little town of Scottsboro. The youths, who ranged in age from thirteen to nineteen, had been jumping trains across northern Alabama, looking for work in the midst of the Great Depression, and they had the misfortune to share the freight cars with two white women who concocted a phony story that they had been raped. Within less than a week after their arrest, eight of the nine had been sentenced to die in Alabama's electric chair. The all-white jury deadlocked in the case of the youngest black teenager after several jurors refused to accept the prosecutor's recommendation for a life sentence. (Seven of the jurors demanded the electric chair for the thirteen-year-old.)

Although I had hoped, as I said in the preface to my book, to explain something of what that nightmare meant to those nine black teenagers caught in the web of white injustice, it now seems dated and hesitant in its attempts to probe the inner meaning of the experience for them and for other African Americans. Whatever narrative momentum the story developed lay in my efforts to understand the destructive impulses that led white Southerners—many of them decent, God-fearing, and kindly people—to countenance the most brutal and inhumane acts.

My second book moved back three quarters of a century, to the aftermath of the great war between North and South—as my grandfather called it, the "War of Northern Aggression." In *When the War Was Over*, I tried to examine the ways in which white Southern leaders responded to defeat and emancipation. But the subtext was much the same. Through the years I continued to write and to work with documentary filmmakers, but inevitably I kept returning to the same theme: the fears and hatreds which ignited the legal persecution of the nine Scottsboro defendants and which had served as the foundation for the policies adopted by the white Southern leadership in the aftermath of the Civil War. What compulsion, I kept asking myself, drove my great-grandfather and his brothers and kin and most of the men of his generation to acts that did such harm to the black men and women in their midst.

Most reviewers described *Scottsboro* and *When the War Was Over* as bleak and depressing stories—and they were—but I still believed somewhat when I wrote those books that if I told the story, if people simply grasped the enormity of our nation's heritage of racial oppression and discrimination, they would change. When I began, I wrote with the white-hot passion of anger and indignation. My dissertation adviser reined me in with an instructive warning: "You do not need to browbeat your reader with reminders that this is the story of oppression and discrimination. You need to tell the story as truthfully and as honestly as you can. If those readers have a core of moral sensibility, they will understand what you are saying. If they don't, a thousand harangues about injustice will not amount to anything." Once I gained control of my anger, I concluded that George Tindall was right. I believed with great passion in the power of the story. I believed that truth-telling about our past (and my own past as a white Southerner) could make a difference in shaping people's actions and their commitments.

For years I kept above my desk a quotation from a speech Robert Kennedy had given at the University of Cape Town, South Africa, in 1966, when the only future for that country seemed a bloodbath as whites fought to the death to maintain their privilege and power and black South Africans seemed to confront an equally grim choice: submission to oppression or a death struggle which would leave the country a wasteland. Kennedy confronted that despair head-on. The great danger that all of us face, he said:

Dan T. Carter

is the despairing belief there is nothing one man or one woman can do against the enormous array of the world's ills—against misery and ignorance, injustice and violence. . . . It is true that few will have the greatness to bend history itself; but each of us can work to change a small portion of events. . . .

It is from those numberless diverse acts of courage and belief that human history is shaped. Each time men and women stand up for an ideal, or act to improve the lot of others, or strike out against injustice, they send a tiny ripple of hope—and crossing each other from a million different centers of energy and daring these ripples build a current which can sweep down the mightiest walls of oppression and resistance.

In the giddy days of the mid-1960s—even as late as the election of Jimmy Carter—I still dreamed of a day when a racially healed South might offer to the nation an opportunity for redemption instead of an object lesson in hate. But as the events of the 1970s and 1980s unfolded it was clear that Alabama Governor George Wallace, not Georgia's former president, Jimmy Carter, was the Southerner whose mark had been left upon American society.

Governor Wallace, four-term governor of Alabama and the subject of my recent biography, led the fight for racial segregation through the 1960s and parlayed his notoriety into four presidential campaigns. There was never any likelihood that he would be elected president of the United States; he was too raw, too crude, too Southern. But he had been one of the great transitional figures in American politics, both poltergeist and weather vane in the America of the 1960s and 1970s. His speeches and campaigns combined the traditional conservative agenda—a bellicose foreign policy, low taxes, and a limited federal government—with the new social agenda. It was George Wallace who first articulated the full range of this new political agenda: from anger over the Supreme Court's rejection of prayer in the schools through angry denunciations of busing, from outrage over pornography to resentment over the expenditure of public resources for the poor. The neoconservative political movement of the 1970s and 1980s had many sources, but it was

Reflections of a Reconstructed White Southerner

George Wallace who furnished the passion and paved the way for later politicians. He had foreseen the tide on which Ronald Reagan sailed into the White House. When Wallace retired from public life in 1986, the nation's newspaper of record, the New York Times, argued that it was Wallace who had "sniffed out early the changes America came to know by many names: white backlash . . . the silent majority . . . the alienated voters. . . . "

Most of all, with a skillful use of euphemisms and code words, Wallace had made it possible to use race in a way that would have seemed unthinkable in the mid-1960s. In tracing the line that runs directly from George Wallace's 1963 "Stand in the Schoolhouse Door" to Richard Nixon's "Southern Strategy" through Ronald Reagan's amiable harangues against "welfare queens" to George Bush's use of the Willie Horton case, I have come face to face with the end of most of the naive assumptions that guided my writing for the first twenty years of my career.

And now, with the rise of black separatism, the circle seems to have closed. Recently I heard one of my colleagues slam a door and storm out of his classroom, so angry he was shaking. When he calmed down, he explained that, in an attempt to provoke his passive students, he had sarcastically asked: Why don't we go back to a segregated society? To his stunned amazement, several students took him seriously and began talking about the virtues of racial separation. His white students thought it prevented racial conflict; his black students argued that it gave space against white domination.

Perhaps because, as a white Southerner, I have seen the dark side of tribal self-affirmation, I remain a skeptic. Whenever I see people define themselves by their gender, their "race," their religion, or their culture, I recoil with hostility. However important these forms of self-definition may be in creating a sense of self-worth and "empowerment," they are also powerful building blocks in almost every system of oppression. Our accents, our skin color, our sexuality, our

Dan T. Carter

ethnicity are more than mere veneer, but less than the sum total of our common humanity.

In the end, I am left with the faint hope, rather than the careless assumption, that there is still power in telling a story about our past which speaks to the same issues of moral justice and racial reconciliation. I have continued to tell the stories of heroes, heroines, and villains; but perhaps because I have grown older, perhaps because we live in ambivalent times, I have developed a special empathy for reluctant heroes and heroines.

I have discovered many such individuals, black and white, male and female, in my research, but for some reason I keep returning to the story of a Selma, Alabama, auto dealer, Arthur Lewis. As the civil rights movement escalated in the Alabama river town in 1964 and 1965, Lewis quietly urged local officials to negotiate in good faith with local civil rights leaders; but he did little else, even as he angrily chafed at his own timidity. (He was "yellow," he bitterly confided to one friend.) Like any businessman, he was worried about the likelihood of economic reprisals, particularly since he was Jewish and especially vulnerable to retaliation from professional bigots.

But on the evening of March 7, 1965, he and his wife, Muriel, were watching the televised showing of the film *Judgment at Nuremberg*. At 9:40 EST—the film had been running for almost an hour and a half—Spencer Tracy, who played the gentle but implacable American war crimes judge, was talking with the nervous cook and housekeeper of his rented Nuremberg house, trying to understand how good and decent Germans had allowed the Nazis to flourish, when news anchor Frank Reynolds interrupted to announce a special news bulletin. The Lewises, along with forty-eight million viewers, watched a hastily edited account of the afternoon's events at Selma's Pettus Bridge. They needed no voice-over to explain the horrific footage of state troopers and local sheriff's deputies brutally beating a group of civil

*Reflections of a Reconstructed White Southerner*

rights demonstrators as they crossed Selma's Pettus Bridge in a demonstration against their inability to register to vote.

The next day, in a letter to a group of close friends, the Lewises recounted their efforts to work behind the scenes. "We could be called moderates, but not liberals," they said, "balancing on a very thin tight-rope while trying to do what we believe is right and just." There were "decent people everywhere and this town is no exception," but the time for quiet diplomacy was over. "We must act differently, and think differently."

Within seventy-two hours, local white racist leaders had obtained a copy of the letter, which they edited to make the couple seem more radical and then circulated throughout the city. Arthur and Muriel Lewis had steeled themselves for the hate letters, the threatening telephone calls, and the boycott of their business. What they had not anticipated was the frightened response of community leaders. When Arthur Lewis invited a dozen of the wealthiest and most important white "moderates" to his home, he asked that they sign and publish a document which he called a "Declaration of Good Faith." It was little more than an affirmation that all citizens had the right to be protected from abuse and a pledge to support interracial communication "on a basis of mutual respect"; but the cautious proposal set off weeks of bitter and acrimonious quarreling. Finally, friends of Arthur and Muriel Lewis warned them that they were "tainted" by their "radical" position. The only hope for action was for them to withdraw from any connection with the proposed declaration.

Eventually, the town's business and community leaders—concerned over the economic implications of the continuing image of white resistance—published a watered-down version of the resolution in the local newspaper. Ironically, they received widespread praise from the national media for their "courageous stand," while the role of Arthur and Muriel Lewis was almost ignored. When one of my stu-

49

Dan T. Carter

dents talked to Muriel Lewis not too long ago, there was still pain—and, yes, anger—in her recollection of these events. She never regretted their decision, she said, and neither did her husband as long as he lived. But neither did either have any illusions about the cost involved in taking a stand and the limited impact they had been able to have on an entrenched community leadership committed to maintaining the comfortable status quo.

If I remain committed to the power of the story, the last twenty years of my life has taught me that there are far more meanings in the stories I have told than I ever imagined when I began my career as a historian.

*Reflections of a Reconstructed White Southerner*

# 4. Reflections on Race and Gender Systems

*Darlene Clark Hine is John A. Hannah Professor of American History at Michigan State University. She earned her B.A. at Roosevelt University in 1968 and her M.A. at Kent State University in 1970, where she also received her Ph.D. in 1975. Prior to her appointment at Michigan State, she taught at South Carolina State University, where she was Coordinator of Black Studies, and Purdue University, where for a time she served as vice provost. She also taught at the University of Delaware, where during the 1989–90 academic year she held the appointment of Visiting Distinguished Professor of Women's Studies. She is the author of* Black Victory: The Rise and Fall of the White Primary in Texas *(1979), and* When the Truth Is Told: A History of Black Women's Culture and Community in Indiana, 1875–1950 *(1981). Her study of black nurses,* Black Women in White: Racial Conflict and Cooperation in the Nursing Profession, 1890–1950 *(1989), won numerous awards, including the Lavinia L. Dock Book Award of the American Association for the History of Nurses, and the Gustavus Myers Center Award. She is the editor of* Black Women in America: An Historical Encyclopedia *(1993) and most recently pub-*

*lished* Speak Truth to Power: Black Professional
Class in United States History *(1996). Along with
her many other honors, grants, and fellowships, she has
been an American Council of Learned Societies Fellow and
a National Humanities Center Fellow. Professor Hine is
presently working on studies of African Americans in the
medical and legal professions from 1868 to 1950 and on
a biography of Madam C. J. Walker.*

During the past two decades I have witnessed and par-
ticipated in two of the major paradigmatic shifts that have
transformed American history. The first transformation involved the flowering and legitimatization of black history
as an essential and respected field of study. The second shift
signaled the maturation and entrenchment of women's history. Neither process is complete. My concentration on reclaiming, researching, and publishing the history of black
women in the United States requires that I straddle both
fields. Just as race became a major conceptual category in
the writing of the recent generation of American historians,
so too must gender analysis achieve the same widespread
acceptance. Black women's history begs an analysis empha-
sizing the connectedness of race and gender systems of
domination and the resistance they provoked. But before
discussing my scholarship and the impact that the black
American struggle for social justice and first class citizenship had on it, I will reflect on how and why I chose to
become a historian and trace the evolution of my thinking
about black women's history as an integral part of African
American history.

If my uncle, Dennis Perry, a professor of microbiology at
Northwestern University Medical School in Chicago, had
had a say, I never would have become a historian. Throughout my high school years, Uncle Dennis carefully groomed
me for a career in science. One of the science projects that

*Reflections on Race and Gender Systems*

we worked on actually won me a slot in the 1963 state competition and a showing at the Museum of Science and Industry. For my family and friends the high point of all this was my appearance on a now defunct CBS television show named, I believe, *Science Today*, where I demonstrated how to detect and eliminate the odorless, colorless, and tasteless deadly gas, carbon monoxide. I have been trying to identify and eradicate noxious substances ever since, racism and sexism being the most lethal of all.

While an undergraduate at Roosevelt University my interest in science was replaced by a more passionate embrace of history. I was shaped, in many ways, by the Black Arts, or Black Consciousness Movement with its celebration of music, art, theater, poetry, and search for an empowering black identity. In keeping with the quest for a more "authentic identity," I become the first on my block and in my family to declare that black was beautiful. I cut the permanent out of my hair and wore it Afro style and donned cowrie shell earrings. I lectured my parents on the perils of eating pork and voting Republican. I applauded the graduate students who, like John Bracey and James Turner, boldly critiqued the European bias in our education and demanded that black history be taught as an integral part of the curriculum. With impatient urgency, we demanded that predominantly white institutions of higher education launch Black Studies programs, hire more black professors, and interact more positively with black communities. Through this tumultuous period, one thing rankled me most. I was bothered by an inability to explain white fear and black anger. I knew it had something to do with racism, but I had no understanding of its foundation, causes, or cure.

Actually, much of what I learned about racism, race relations, and the differences between political and cultural nationalisms was gleaned from conversations with fellow students, outside of the classroom, and through reading the books that passed from hand to hand. I devoured many of the most popular texts, including Frantz Fanon's *The Wretched*

Darlene Clark Hine

of the Earth (1963); *The Autobiography of Malcolm X* (1965); LeRoi Jones's, now Amiri Baraka's *Preface to a Twenty Volume Suicide Note*; the plays of Ed Bullins; and the poetry of Don Lee, now Haki R. Madhubuti; and the works of other writers published by Broadside Press and by Third World Press. I was transfixed by the paintings and poster art of Murry N. DePillars. I attended meetings of the Nation of Islam and once heard the honorable Elijah Muhammad speak. As I grew into blackness, I tried to figure out what I could do, how I could also make a meaningful and useful contribution in the whole struggle for social justice.

As I attended guest lectures by historian John Hope Franklin on campus and heard Lerone Bennett, John Henrik Clarke, and others at locations throughout the city in churches, museums, and community centers, I developed an appreciation for history's capacity to explain why things are. I wanted to know and I wanted that knowledge to have a definite structure. I elected to become a historian, and I took every course historian Hollis Lynch offered. He subsequently became my adviser and helped me to select a graduate school. I remember being very impressed with Lynch's work in the history of pan-Africanism. I learned from linguist Lorenzo Dow Turner all about Africanisms in Gullah dialect. I read *Black Power* and listened closely to everything political science professor Charles V. Hamilton had to say. One of the most respected and admired of my professors was sociologist St. Clair Drake. I, like countless other undergraduates, sat around him in the school cafeteria, soaking up his wisdom, basking in his intelligence and renown, and listening to his endless stories about black Chicago.

Following Roosevelt University I continued my studies at Kent State University and studied with historian August Meier. The period from 1964 to 1968 proved to be the most volatile and transformative years in the Chicago civil rights era. Martin Luther King, Jr., took up temporary residence in the windy city. In 1965 Congress enacted voting rights legislation, thus signaling a successful conclusion of one aspect

*Reflections on Race and Gender Systems*

of the civil rights struggle. Shortly thereafter the Black Power movement exploded on the national scene. In 1966 I taped to my bedroom door and committed to memory the Black Panther Party platform and program of "what we want, what we believe." Five of the points still resonate almost thirty years later:

> 1. We want freedom. We want power to determine the destiny of our Black Community. . . . 2. We want full employment for our people. . . . 3. We want an end to the robbery by the capitalists of our Black Community. . . . 4. We want decent housing, fit for shelter of human beings. . . . 5. We want education for our people that exposes the true nature of this decadent American society. We want education that teaches us our true history and our role in present-day society.[1]

It was the fifth plank in the platform that affected me. I reasoned that if black Americans were to be taught "our true history" then obviously someone would have to research and write it. I had found my role in the black struggle; I would become a historian.

In 1967 rebellions erupted in Detroit and in dozens of major urban areas. In April 1968 Chicago's black community exploded in the wake of the assassination of Dr. Martin Luther King, Jr. On December 4, 1969, Chicago policemen murdered Black Panther leaders Fred Hampton and Mark Clark during a predawn raid. A commission, headed by NAACP executive secretary Roy Wilkins and former attorney general Ramsey Clark, investigated the murders and issued a strongly worded report reaffirming Hampton's and Clark's humanity. Wilkins and Ramsey Clark declared that the legal system had failed to protect the lives and rights of the slain Panthers. Further, the police who planned the raid were never indicted: "Fred Hampton and Mark Clark were valuable young men. They could have enriched our lives. If they spoke of violence, suffered it, or used it, we should not be surprised. It was not foreign to their environment, nor did their government eschew it. And talented or not, violent or nonviolent, they were human beings whose lives and le-

Darlene Clark Hine

gal rights must be cherished by a just society." I was at graduate school when the raid and the commission's inquiry took place, and I followed the course of events with special interest. It seemed as if only months before I had heard Clark and Hampton speak at Roosevelt University. They were the first activists with whom I had identified to die in the struggle.[2]

The death of the Chicago Panthers affected me deeply, but the experiences of my generation were far from over. On May 4, 1970, I stood on the grassy slope with other students and faculty at Kent State University and watched Ohio National Guardsmen massacre white student anti-war protesters. A few days later I heard of the Jackson State University killings. These accumulated deaths challenged my conviction that the study of the past and the doing of history was an effective way to understand the present. Yet, I held on to the belief that history would provide a way of understanding events that increasingly made little sense. With the same intense fervor that I had buried myself in black culture and consciousness, I now turned to history. John Hope Franklin's words, though uttered over a decade later, capture well my thinking at that time:

> Every generation has the opportunity to write its own history, and indeed it is obliged to do so. Only in that way can it provide its contemporaries with the materials vital to understanding the present and to planning strategies for coping with the future. Only in that way can it fulfill its obligation to pass on to posterity the accumulated knowledge and wisdom of the past, which, after all, give substance and direction for the continuity of civilization.[3]

The desire to understand the present by studying the past informed my decision to follow August Meier's lead and to focus my research on questions of race relations. My revised dissertation, *Black Victory: The Rise and Fall of the White Primary in Texas* (Millwood, N.Y.: KTO, 1979), reflected a fascination with the pre–civil rights movement generation of activists and the legal strategies that black and white lawyers of the NAACP devised to overthrow constitutionally sanctioned

*Reflections on Race and Gender Systems*

disfranchisement. The topic satisfied a gnawing curiosity about the connections between social protest, individual action, and mass mobilization. Arguably, the NAACP was the most successful model of interracial cooperation in modern American history. The organization's history provided ample proof that black and white Americans could work together successfully toward the goal of social justice for all, that past differences need not dictate our destiny as a nation.

As research on the dissertation progressed, the structures and ideologies of racial exclusion and white supremacy as worked out by white Southern lawyers, judges, and legislators captured my imagination. I pondered why they labored so assiduously to eliminate black Southerners from the political process and effectively manipulated the legal system to justify and sustain that perversion of justice. Forays into this murky terrain uncovered a vanguard of black lawyers, Charles H. Houston, William H. Hastie, and Thurgood Marshall, and an array of lesser known but equally courageous attorneys in local communities throughout the South. The discovery of this cadre of social change agents—less dramatic than the Black Panthers, to be sure—who were the immediate forerunners of the activists of my generation cemented my embrace of history. Fortunately, August Meier insisted that I avoid reading the present into the past and forego hero worship in order to more clearly assess and record the deeds and visions of the early NAACP lawyers.

Any discussion of the role of black lawyers in the war against Jim Crow must begin with Harvard Law School graduate Charles Hamilton Houston, who likened the black lawyer to a "social engineer." Throughout the 1930s and the 1940s and until his death in 1950, Houston worked zealously to eradicate the evil of racial segregation and to cleanse the United States Constitution of its acceptance and defense of inequality as evidenced in key U.S. Supreme Court decisions in 1883 and in 1896. Houston imbued dozens of young black lawyers, many of whom he trained while dean of Howard University Law School, with a passion and heart-

Darlene Clark Hine

felt determination to use the legal system against itself. His prize student and future United States Supreme Court Justice, Thurgood Marshall, continued his legacy and with consummate skill successfully persuaded the Supreme Court in case after case to destroy the legal basis for inequality in America. Before their onslaught, the white primary fell in *Smith v. Allwright* in 1944; residential restrictive covenants bit the dust in *Shelley v. Kramer* in 1948; and segregated law schools went the way of the dinosaurs in *Sweatt v. Painter* in 1950.

Charles Houston was a visionary. He and Marshall believed that the decisions of the U.S. Supreme Court in the aftermath of Reconstruction had thwarted the prime objectives of the Fourteenth and Fifteenth Amendments to the Constitution. In a dedicated, relentless style that begs admiration, these black lawyers struggled to restore the original intentions of the framers of the Reconstruction amendments. Houston, Hastie, and Marshall held fast to the conviction that the Fourteenth Amendment was designed to promote the equality of African Americans and was not simply a tool designed to protect the property and promote the well-being of whites and their corporate entities. The collective vision of black NAACP attorneys was that American law could be transformed and infused with a deeper respect for the rights of all people, especially African Americans.

I learned some critical lessons from studying the lives and thoughts of the men behind the white primary cases. I came to appreciate that history could correct erroneous perceptions of social activists as either deviants or bourgeois sellouts. In fact, from my study of the NAACP lawyers of the 1930s and 1940s I discovered that the most transformative, or remedial, social deeds are often the actions of well-adjusted, brilliant individuals who possess an oppositional consciousness and a mastery of the skills essential to their chosen profession. Houston and the others demonstrated that they were able to critique their society, offer an alternative vision, and implement plans and strategies to obliter-

*Reflections on Race and Gender Systems*

ate oppressive systems of power relations. To put the message in more contemporary terms, I learned that it is indeed possible to dismantle the master's house using the master's tools if you have your head screwed on straight. I am drawn to the analytical model George Lipsitz developed in his examination of civil rights activist Ivory Perry. Lipsitz argues that,

> while activism involves pain and stress, it is not primarily an expression of personal discomfort but an outgrowth of an individual's analysis and understanding of collective discomfort. It expresses a logical and collectively sanctioned response to hierarchy and exploitation on the part of strong-willed individuals with clear and comforting connections to networks of opposition.[4]

As will become apparent shortly, Lipsitz's observations make an appropriate lead-in to a discussion of the work that I have been engaged in for the past fourteen years, the study of black women's history. In 1980, the year after I published *Black Victory*, I decided to investigate the history of African Americans in the professions. My work on black lawyers had sparked an interest in their professional counterparts in medicine, science, and education. I wanted to know if they had engaged in similar struggles for social justice that laid the foundation upon which Martin Luther King, Jr., and the leaders of the modern civil rights movement would stand. Initially I focused on the history of blacks in the medical profession, but the work was interrupted early on and still awaits completion. Little did I suspect that the call from Shirley Herd, a school teacher in Indianapolis who was president of the local chapter of the National Council of Negro Women, would have such a profound impact on the trajectory and content of my scholarship and would lead to the 1989 publication of *Black Women in White: Racial Conflict and Cooperation in the Nursing Profession, 1890 to 1950*, and the 1993 appearance of *Black Women in America: An Historical Encyclopedia*.

When Herd invited me to write a history of black women in Indiana for her organization, I refused, explaining that I knew nothing about black women's history and had never taken any courses in the subject. She was nonplussed, rejoining with a series of questions that forced me to remember why I had become a historian in the first place. "Let me get this straight," she said. "You are a black woman? You are a historian?" And when I replied yes, she challenged, "You mean to tell me that you can't put those two things together and write us a history of black women in Indiana?"

Herd's questions disconcerted me and eventually prompted me to connect my biography with my profession, to forge an integrated identity that equally emphasized my race, gender, and work. It was within this framework that I did her bidding and wrote the short book *When the Truth Is Told: A History of Black Women's Culture and Community in Indiana, 1875–1950* (1981). The long-term impact of our relationship on my consciousness and scholarship is clearly evident. In 1980 we (historian Patrick Bidelman, Shirley Herd, and Virtea Downey) received a grant from the National Endowment for the Humanities for the Black Women in the Middle West project. It was while engaged in the work to create a Midwestern black women's archive that I came to understand more completely the problems with history. The very process of reclaiming past records and documents of ignored, excluded, distorted, and stereotyped black women gave me many insights into the power of history and the sexual and racial politics of historical construction. Historians decide who is meritorious, what events should be documented and taught, and how things and individuals are to be known and remembered.

Propitiously, this entry into black women's history underscored the largely unacknowledged importance of black women's clubs and organizations to black American communities. Beginning with their national mobilization impulse in the 1890s and the creation of the National Association of Colored Women's clubs (NACW), to the 1935 founding of the National Council of Negro Women, black women formed a vital network that laid the institutional foundation undergirding most of their social reform, community uplift, and self-improvement work. The motto of NACW clubs, "Lifting as We Climb," succinctly captured all of the myriad dimensions of the modern civil rights mobilization movement. Yet, the motto also conveyed the women's consciousness of the complex and interconnected nature of the struggle against racial, sexual, and class systems of domination.

The reclamation of the history of black women in the early 1980s coincided with events taking place in the larger historical profession. At the precise moment that I was working on the Black Women in the Middle West project I was invited by the teaching division of the American Historical Association to organize a conference, "The State of Afro-American History, Past, Present, and Future." The assessment or inventory conference, held at Purdue University in 1983, signaled the legitimization of the field of African American history. We divided the field into three topical areas—slavery, emancipation, and urban studies. At the conclusion of the conference the advisory committee acknowledged that the least developed area in the field of black history was black women's history. Black women remained virtually invisible to most professional historians. At best they occupied a shadowy space in historical monographs and in American history survey textbooks that usually limited discussion of black women to Phillis Wheatley, Sojourner Truth, and Harriet Tubman. Accordingly, I was charged with the responsibility for preparing a synthesis of existing scholarship and for identifying the topics and themes in need of more scholarly attention.

The resulting essay, "Lifting the Veil, Shattering the Silence: Black Women's History in Slavery and Freedom," was included in the proceedings volume that I edited, *The State of Afro-American History, Past, Present, and Future* (1986). The essay underscored that black women's history was just beginning to emerge within women's and Afro-American history and stressed the need for much more attention. I traced the con-

Darlene Clark Hine

tours of the field and assessed its prospects by synthesizing the current literature and by examining the following themes: sex roles and female networks, the black family, work, religion, social reform, and creative expressions. The amount of scholarship on black women was so limited that in 1983 one could accomplish all of the things delineated in twenty-five pages. Within ten years a virtual revolution had taken place in African American history, and today the study of black women is flourishing.

Since 1983, scholars have begun the difficult task of looking beyond the surface and penetrating what I call black women's culture of dissemblance. My discussion of the culture of dissemblance is a theory of difference that helps to explicate our understanding of how knowledge about black women is generated and yet simultaneously shielded from the hostile scrutiny of others, especially white men and women, but also black men and children. In other words, not all of the invisibility of black women in the historical record was due to the blindness or racism and sexism of historians. Many black women quite deliberately engaged in behaviors designed to protect their interior lives and to create space to be themselves. An often heard refrain was the caution, "Don't put your business in the streets." Simply put, there were many aspects of black women's lives that they simply did not wish to be known.

Another distinct theme that runs through the thirty essays and the books on the history of black women in the nursing profession and in the Middle West is the ever present consciousness of resistance. Black women defined resistance as being integral to survival, not only on an individual but on a community level. The resistance may have been passive, active, overt, covert, ambivalent, focused, and/or diffused. Collectively all black women's forms of resistance constituted a rejection of society's stereotyped images and negative depictions of their womanhood. As long as the larger society viewed them as immoral and unworthy of respect, they could be dehumanized, rejected, made powerless, and subjected to racial and sexual domination. The struggle of black women had, of necessity, to be nuanced and multi-faceted.

In hindsight, I am struck by how consumed I was throughout the 1960s and 1970s with questions of race and race relations. Throughout my college education and the early years of my career as a professional historian, questions of race dominated virtually every intellectual conversation I had with friends. The historian Evelyn Brooks Higginbotham persuasively argues that the metalanguage of race silences all other discourses.[5] This was certainly true of my personal intellectual history. I rarely considered or formulated questions related to the historical and social construction of gender and class. Rather, I distinctly remember engaging in misguided and ill-informed discussions about the absence of a class structure within black America. Black women, of course, were neither objects nor subjects of history. They existed outside of history. During these formative decades of my consciousness, black history had race but no gender. I dare say that all would-be historians of African American history lacked a vocabulary with which to discuss gender.

The transformation of American history is far from complete and many questions still need to be addressed. Yet there is, perhaps, reason for optimism. There now exists a vocabulary of gender, accessible reference books, and several major black women's history archives. Since the publication of *Black Women in America: An Historical Encyclopedia*, all discourse in black history has changed. To make an encyclopedia is to claim a historiographical moment. The encyclopedia of black women in American history exposes the state of black women's history while suggesting issues, themes, and individuals ripe for future exploration and analysis. A virtual revolution had to take place in African American and in women's history, as well as in the new social history, before black women historians could claim the voice and space for subjects who warrant a hearing at the bar of his-

Darlene Clark Hine

tory. This is the revolution in which the *Encyclopedia* participates and which it challenges.

Ironically, my work has now come full circle. I am once again drawn to study the contributions of black lawyers in the quest for civil rights. There are, however, striking differences. When I began my career as a professional historian, I studied the process of social change and focused specifically on the history of the NAACP. This work led me to delve more deeply into the lives and careers of black lawyers. Now my interest in the larger professional class has expanded to include not only black lawyers but educators, physicians, scientists, and nurses. An examination of the process of professionalization invariably led me back to civil rights questions, of course, complicated by race, class, and gender constructions and intersections. Black men and women professionals were severely restricted by the operation of Jim Crow laws. Yet, these were precisely the black Americans most capable of protesting against discrimination and segregation through mobilization within and across class lines. I suspect that a greater understanding of their strategies may provide critical insight into and inspiration for today's activists in the ongoing struggle for social justice and the elimination of race, sex, and class systems of hierarchy and domination.

NOTES

1. For the record, I include the five remaining points of the Panther platform and program. "6. We want all Black men to be exempt from military service. . . . 7. We want an immediate end to POLICE BRUTALITY and MURDER of Black people. . . . 8. We want freedom for all Black men held in federal, state, county and city prisons and jails. . . . 9. We want all Black people when brought to trial to be tried in court by a jury of their peer group or people from their Black communities, as defined by the Constitution of the United States. . . . 10. We want land, bread, housing, education, clothing, justice, and peace. And as our ma-

*Reflections on Race and Gender Systems*

jor political objective, a United Nations supervised plebiscite to be held throughout the Black colony in which only Black colonial subjects will be allowed to participate, for the purpose of determining the will of Black people as to their national destiny."

2. "Search and Destroy: A Report by the Commission of Inquiry into the Black Panthers and the Police," Roy Wilkins and Ramsey Clark, Chairmen of the Commission of Inquiry into the Panthers and the Police; reprinted in *The Eyes on the Prize Civil Rights Reader*, ed. Clayborne Carson, David J. Garrow, Gerald Gill, Vincent Harding, and Darlene Clark Hine (New York: Penguin Books, 1991), p. 519.

3. John Hope Franklin, "On the Evolution of Scholarship in Afro-American History," in *The State of Afro-American History: Past, Present, and Future*, ed. Darlene Clark Hine (Baton Rouge: Louisiana State University Press, 1987), p. 13.

4. George Lipsitz, *A Life in the Struggle: Ivory Perry and the Culture of Opposition* (Philadelphia: Temple University Press, 1988), p. 18.

5. Evelyn Brooks Higginbotham, "African-American Women's History and the Metalanguage of Race," *Signs* 17 (Winter 1992): 251–74.

DAVID LEVERING LEWIS

# 5. From Eurocentrism to Polycentrism

David Levering Lewis is Martin Luther King, Jr., University Professor at Rutgers, The State University of New Jersey in New Brunswick. He earned his B.A. at Fisk University in 1956, his M.A. at Columbia University in 1958, and his Ph.D. at the London School of Economics and Political Science in 1962. Prior to assuming his chair at Rutgers in 1985, Professor Lewis taught at several other institutions, including the University of the District of Columbia and the University of California, San Diego. Among his many publications are King: A Critical Biography (1970), Prisoners of Honor: The Dreyfus Affair (1975), When Harlem Was in Vogue (1981), and The Race to Fashoda: European Colonialism and African Resistance in the Scramble for Africa (1988). His most recent book W. E. B. Du Bois: Biography of a Race, 1868–1919 (1993) has earned him the Bancroft Prize, the Francis Parkman Prize, and the Pulitzer Prize in Biography. He has held fellowships from the Guggenheim Foundation, the National Humanities Center, the Center for Advanced Study in the Behavioral Sciences, and the Woodrow Wilson International Center for Scholars. Professor

*Lewis is presently completing the second volume of his life of Du Bois.*

In his fecund essay, "On the Evolution of Scholarship in Afro-American History," John Hope Franklin describes a fourth generation of scholars that came of age after 1970. "No area of inquiry escaped their inquiry," writes Franklin in *The State of Afro-American History*, edited by Darlene Clark Hine. "They worked on the colonial period, the era of Reconstruction, and the twentieth century. They examined slavery, the Afro-American family, and antebellum free blacks. Their range was wide. . . . "[1] This was a relatively populous generation, well-trained in the best research universities, interracial in composition, and ambitious in the scope of its investigations. The first generation had produced George Washington Williams; the second included W. E. B. Du Bois, Carter G. Woodson, and Charles Wesley; it was succeeded after 1950 by the third generation of Rayford Logan, Herbert Aptheker, Helen Edmonds, August Meier, Benjamin Quarles, and John Hope Franklin himself.[2]

To describe the fourth generation as something of a jumble of untamed egoes, conflicting paradigms and research agendas, and extreme variations in standards is not entirely unwarranted. One gets an appreciation of this burgeoning and increasingly contentious universe of new scholarship in *Black History and the Historical Profession*, the anecdotally rich and analytically uneven collection of interviews with scholars in African American history published by August Meier and Elliott Rudwick in the mid-80s. This generation of students of Negro, Black, and now African American life and history is my own generation: that of John Blassingame, Mary Berry, Nell Painter, Eugene Genovese, Nathan Huggins, Herbert Gutman, and Thomas Holt, to mention randomly a very few. Meier and Rudwick place me squarely within it, writing that "the first published books in Afro-

David Levering Lewis

American history by this new crop of black historians appeared quite suddenly—between 1970 and 1972 with the arrival of David Lewis's *King: A Critical Biography.* . . . " Mine, it seems, was one of the first of the new investigations into problems of leadership (along with Louis Harlan's *Booker T. Washington*) that moved African American biography into the rigorously contextual place where it now resides with such accomplished practitioners as Wilson Moses, Stephen Fox, Kenneth Manning, Dickson Bruce, Waldo Martin, Taylor Branch, and Arnold Rampersad.[3]

Rather surprisingly, it had not really registered that at least superficially my career makes an admirable fit for membership in Franklin's fourth cohort of scholars. I confess that, until this invitation to talk about myself and the discipline of history, I had given only occasional and casual thought to what brought me into the profession, to why I have ranged so broadly as almost to render myself suspect in the eyes of some of my more austerely orthodox peers, and finally, and more dauntingly, to how the writing of history may serve some social purpose. A curious deficit in introspection is commonplace among professional historians, I think—a function of the inductive way we do history and of the temperamental aversion most of us develop over time to theorizing about the value of what we do. To paraphrase Henry Ford, many of us think theory in history is bunk. And yet, to indulge another paraphrase, is the unexamined historian's life worth living? Examining my career, then, I find myself constrained to admit that I would have been incredulous and even disconcerted thirty-odd years ago when I emerged from graduate school if some seer had predicted a modicum of distinction in the field of African American history. For my nurturing—both familial and intellectual—was what could be characterized as resolutely mainstream, majoritarian, assimilationist—Eurocentric, in today's argot.

As the youngest son in a secure and relatively affluent, two-parent household, as a carefully encouraged pupil

68

From Eurocentrism to Polycentrism

speeding through high school in two years, and as a confident collegian who experimented with a semester of law school before deciding to try graduate schools in New York and London, I emerged from these experiences minted as pure Talented Tenth. My earliest memories go back to the cloistered college community in Wilberforce, Ohio, and to a long parade of academic, ministerial, civil rights, and other worthies sitting down to and rising sufficed from the family dinner table. Those were racially segregated times, when accommodations even in the best northern hotels were problematic, and African American movers and shakers relied on the nearest middle-class households for hospitality. Memory tends to inflate in such matters, but I think I don't much exaggerate in saying that many past and future dissertation subjects in African American history came to our home— Adam Clayton Powell, Jr., W. E. B. Du Bois, Marian Anderson, Walter White, Channing Tobias, and Thurgood Marshall come to mind.

Our household lore was freighted with vivid—often breathtaking—accounts of skirmishes along the color line (some of them narrated by the principals themselves). I recall especially the stories my father would tell about a shining moment when, as the principal of Little Rock's colored high school, he had sacrificed his career to testify on behalf of the teachers' salary equalization suit filed by the NAACP, successfully argued by the young Thurgood Marshall. There was an article by Du Bois about the case in the *Chicago Defender* for June 14, 1947. It said that my even-tempered father had exploded: "And they say that he told those white members of the Board of Education facts which they have never forgotten. What happened? The wages were equalized, but he lost his job. He is now on meagre salary in the North."[4] The piece was read to me more than a few times. Now it might be supposed that this was an environment ideally conducive to preoccupation with the past, present, and future of the Negro, as we said then. Surely, this had to be a crucible in which pride of race was hardened and shaped,

David Levering Lewis

one in which a determined hunger was formed to learn about the African past here and in the home continent. As it developed, however, the reverse tended to be true.

My father's library contained Du Bois's *Black Folk Then and Now*, Woodson's *The Story of the Negro Retold*, and even Joel A. Rogers's wildly speculative book, *World's Greatest Men of African Descent*. I dipped into them, but somehow they failed to hold my attention. What they contained was already too familiar in an informal sense. I simply took it for granted that people of African descent had a past full of peaks and troughs. The ancient kingdom of Ghana, the Battle of Adua, and much of Reconstruction were peaks. The Congress of Berlin, *Dred Scott*, and *Plessy v. Ferguson* were chasms. I had my heroes: Septimus Severus, Pushkin, Alexandre Dumas, Benjamin Banneker, and Frederick Douglass. There were a few scoundrels: Iago, Aunt Jemima, and, of course, Booker T. Washington, but not, I admit, Amos and Andy. Steeped in the contributionist historiography of the family dinner table, I came into my teens unaware that most Americans—black as well as white—were unaware of the key facts and main outlines of Negro history.

Yet in appearing to take our past for granted, we middle-class blacks were also profoundly insecure about how others perceived our cultural and intellectual endowments—very touchy about the degree to which we succeeded in being accepted as sophisticated citizens. My family and its circle were like characters in a Jessie Fauset novel—committed integrationists whose demeaning and demoralizing existence at the margins of Mainstream America we interpreted as worse than a crime—it was a social absurdity, yet an absurdity we passionately believed to be susceptible of attenuation through exemplary feats of professional or intellectual breakthrough. We were self-consciously what Nell Painter has called "representative Negroes," ever ready to be invited to dinner. However superficial, Willard B. Gatewood's *Aristocrats of Color* gets it exactly right: "Reluctant even in the face of hardening racial lines and the triumphant march of Jim

From Eurocentrism to Polycentrism

Crow to abandon hopes for first-class citizenship and as-similation into American society," it concludes, "they were often in the vanguard of efforts to thwart movements that they believed would perpetuate a segregated society."[5] Thus one badge of civic and social eligibility for us was that of mastering the history that white Americans claimed as their own.

And so it was the key facts and main outlines of other histories that I found most intriguing. Especially ancient history and European history. Marching across almost an entire shelf in our library were the multiple, leather-bound volumes of a lavishly illustrated world history. I spent hours turning those high-gloss pages, following the course of history through wars from Salamis to Sedan. I plowed through the abridged *Decline and Fall of the Roman Empire* by age twelve. Baseball appealed somewhat (as a southpaw I was a natural pitcher), but the real high came with Carlyle's *French Revolution*. The chapter on the flight of Louis and Marie Antoinette to Varennes in that great berlin swaying across the French countryside I thought was the finest piece of history writing ever done. When family fortunes took us from Wilberforce, Ohio, to Atlanta and me from the college laboratory school straight into the sophomore year at Atlanta's Booker T. Washington High, there was more emphasis on U.S. history—a subject I continued, nevertheless, to find pretty parochial and abbreviated. Unlike Rome or Ancien Regime France, U.S. history was unsatisfying because it had no end. And as for a tax revolt by merchants and gentlemen farmers passing for a real revolution, I was positively disdainful. Bernard Pares's *History of Russia*—now there was a grand and tragic subject of wondrous complexity. Still, I relished reading the Beards' *Rise of American Civilization*.

I went off to college at age fifteen, undecided about a major and almost blase about a career. My father's brother, "Uncle Doc"—a nervous, natty little man who was one of Atlanta's most successful physicians—guaranteed a place in his will and tuition beyond college if I decided to attend medical school. Medicine was never a real temptation, however, especially after two semesters of chemistry. Fisk University in my day possessed an exceptionally strong faculty, especially in the enriched, accelerated Ford Foundation–funded program to which I had been admitted without a high school diploma, along with about thirty other young men and women. Ed Pessen handled the Great Books offering. Bernard Spivack led us from Dante to Ibsen in remorseless deadlines of thrice-weekly commentaries. Aaron Douglas made the history of art a series of exciting probes into questions of aesthetics, patronage, and culture. The brilliant poet Bob Hayden brought Joyce's Dublin into the classroom. Oswald Schrag and Scott Buchanan made us care intensely about the charges against Socrates and the skepticism mess which Hume had left to Kant to try to repair. I would eventually minor in philosophy. David Granick didn't make economics easy for me, but I got enough of it to suspect that it was a science whose principles worked best mainly in model form. A manic August Meier taught a whirlwind two-semester course in Western Civilization from Mesopotamia to the Marshall Plan that left us panting.[6]

As is the way with such turning points, I fell into a history major by chance late in my second year. I had just managed to drop a deadly calculus class before it hurt me. By chance, I followed a friend into a U.S. history class. The professor was a handsome, well-built, short man. He chain-smoked as he walked quickly back and forth, alternately stabbing the air for emphasis or manipulating cigarettes like a baton as he lectured in a nasal New England brogue. Something was said about the textbook's characterization of African Americans in the Revolution. The class was using that dated, beautifully written, racially patronizing classic by John Spencer Bassett. I volunteered a response. Whatever it was, it triggered an animated back and forth with the professor. Afterward, I found myself walking across the campus with him, talking about myself, flattered by his affable indulgence of my opiniativeness, and challenged to

From Eurocentrism to Polycentrism

sign up for the class. I was hooked. Ted Currier was the last of the best of the Mr. Chips breed—a spellbinding lecturer with total recall and a quicksilver mind that made it possible (although not pedagogically legitimate) for him to teach courses in Latin American and Russian history, as well as American history with apparently equal competence. One of the youngest students ever admitted to Harvard's graduate history department, Currier had been at Fisk since he was twenty-two. When I knew him, he was probably in his late fifties. His bachelor abode on the campus was an afterhours' classroom and tavern enveloped in smoke and throbbing with sessions about every conceivable historical topic and most everything else. Currier was fiercely proud of one of his former students named John Hope Franklin, who went on to earn a Harvard Ph.D.

I did history at Fisk, and I relished doing it, but it was the messenger as much as the message that inspired me— the way Currier seemed to annihilate the time distance between us and the eras under review in morning classes. "Now where did we leave off? Lewis, King, Miss Reed" (who became transportation secretary Hazel Reed O'Leary), he would ask at the beginning of each lecture, lighting up while each of us flipped through our notes. But not even Ted Currier could fully win me over to American history. For my honors thesis and what I thought was my farewell to history I wrote a massive paper on Arnold Toynbee, and was crushed when Currier mailed it to me after graduation with the terse comment that it might have been a good deal shorter. There was no time to brood, though. I was off to law school at the University of Michigan. I did well enough; but I withdrew after a semester to the consternation of my parents, who deplored the modest lifestyle awaiting me as a college professor and terminated their financial support. I took a train to New York, bunked with a friend from Pomona College, and talked my way in to see Jacques Barzun, then Columbia's dean of arts and sciences. It was the winter of 1957–58, the salad days of higher education when

David Levering Lewis

there were low-interest graduate school loans which were forgiven altogether if the borrower earned his degree in the minimum time possible.

With a loan okayed by Barzun and a live-in job taking care of a lively married couple afflicted by cerebral palsy, I plunged back into history, elated by the experience of the university's famous entry-level course in historiography. But my timing was bad. It was mid-year and Shepherd Clough's seminar in modern French history was full and well underway. The best I could do if I chose not to wait for the next cycle was to gain permission to work immediately on a master's degree in U.S. history with Richard B. Morris— hardly a poor consolation prize. My thesis would have been ideal for Richard Hofstadter, Columbia's most popular historian and, therefore, unavailable to take on any more candidates. I submitted the finished thesis, "John Fiske: A Transitional Figure in American Social Darwinism," to Richard Morris in April 1958. Harvard historian and librarian, the hugely overweight Fiske emerged as one of the nineteenth century's premier public intellectuals, the American avatar of Herbert Spencer's ideas. Yet he unwittingly undermined the materialistic determinism at the center of Spencerianism through an irrepressible American optimism and faith in human agency. My master's thesis confirmed a temperamental preference for social history with a decided intellectual skew mediated through biography. A penchant for irony and paradox was also reinforced.

Meanwhile, I had kept my hand in European history at Columbia, winning a rather grudging 'A' in curmudgeonly Fritz Stern's exigent history of modern Germany and stretching myself in John Hine Mundy's exquisitely presented Age of Philip Augustus. I actually deceived myself for a short time into regretting that my Latin and German were inadequate to allow me to specialize in medieval history. Before throwing in the medieval towel, nevertheless, I wrote a tour de force essay—my first A-plus in graduate school. Once again, I was drawn to reflect upon the paradox of ideas. The subject of the essay was Ernst Kantorowicz's *Frederick II*—an ambitious iconology both of this Jewish historian admired by Hitler and of *Stupor Mundi*, the last Hohenstaufen emperor. Two years later—it must have been summer 1961—I ran into John Mundy and his jaunty beret on the steps of the Bibliothèque Nationale. He immediately recalled the Kantorowicz paper and asked where my academic interests had led. Away from U.S. history and into the French Third Republic, I said over a cup of toxic coffee and the adamantine *sandwich jambon*, then standard issue in the little cafés off the rue Richelieu.

At the time, I seldom gave anything but an occasional, amused thought to the article I had written with August Meier in summer 1958. Running into me at Columbia one day, he had talked in his usual explosive way of a scheme to write a multigenerational study of upper-class African Americans. When Augie explained that his problem was that he had no way of getting into the world of upper-class African Americans, I asked, "Who are these people?" And when it became obvious that he meant folks in Atlanta, I invited him to spend the summer there as the guest of the family. Augie was a sensation as the two of us interviewed virtually every lawyer, physician, banker, college administrator, and pouter pigeon clubwoman in the city. Literally on my way to the ship going to Europe, I stopped off at Meier's New Jersey home where we put the data into prose for the first article of its kind on class structure in Afro-America. "History of the Negro Upper Class in Atlanta, Georgia, 1890–1950" appeared in the spring 1959 issue of the *Journal of Negro Education*.[7] My mother wrote to me in England that she was scandalized by the article's candor. Aside from pride in coauthoring my first publication at twenty-two, I really missed the enduring significance of what we had done. Certainly, I gave no thought to further work along these lines.

After Columbia came the London School of Economics and in rapid succession a tutor in political philosophy—the

David Levering Lewis

renowned K. B. Smelly—and one in French history—the distinguished William Pickles. Pickles and his wife were then much in the news for having produced the first English translation of the constitution of the new Fifth Republic. Bill Pickles was actually very dry, but his course in French Political Thought had snap and crackle for me because of the French political thinkers I was introduced to there through Henri Michel's monumental *L'Idée de l'Etat* and Roger Soltau's brilliantly schematic *French Political Thought in the Nineteenth Century*. Looking back, though, I now see that my fascination with French thought was already well primed due to the precocity of one of my college classmates and best friends. Preston King had gone straight to the London School of Economics from Fisk in 1956. I had followed Preston's dazzling studies through a steady stream of letters. When his master's thesis on Fourier, Proudhon, and Sorel was awarded a rare distinction and the London publisher Frank Cass chose it for one of his first imprints, Preston had sent it to me asking for a general reaction and a title. I read Preston's master's with admiration and envy as I wrote my own John Fiske study. My suggested title for its published incarnation was "Power and Fragmentation." It was soon published as *Fear of Power*.[8]

Reading modern French history and politics with Bill Pickles turned out to be graduate school nirvana. After two trimesters of lectures, tutorials, and fabulously rewarding hours reading in the old British Museum and its Colindale newspaper archive, I went off to Paris to research a dissertation, returning to LSE during the next year and a half for monthly tutorials with Pickles. Much of that period I lived in Versailles, on rue de l'Orangerie, with a delightful royalist family hard by the chateau. The experience did wonders for my French, for my insights into those social and political cleavages cherished by French people across the generations—those chronic tensions between *la droite et la gauche*, traditional France versus modernizing France—*le Pays réel contre le Pays legal*. And for my ego, there was the youngest

From Eurocentrism to Polycentrism

daughter, a Sorbonnarde, who often joined me after a day's research for a cheap Vietnamese meal before we took the train back to Versailles. I had headed for Paris with an elaborately written but actually quite inchoate proposal that read something like "The Political Face of Catholic Modernism in France after the First War." What I had in mind was a lot of broad reading in order to trace the intellectual and political currents discharged by the early nineteenth-century priest, Félicité de Lamennais. As I saw it, the Catholic Church's failure to make its peace with the twentieth century was a story encased in the history of France's Third Republic. Leo XIII's *Rerum Novarum* encyclical and Charles Peguy and Marc Sangnier's politics had succumbed to the reaction spearheaded by Charles Maurras's *Action Française*. But the modernizing tradition was resilient, as the worker priest phenomenon after the Second World War showed.

I chose a biographical topic for a dissertation, once again aiming to use an interesting life as a window opening onto the regnant ideas and movements of a period—biography as historical metaphor, I should have said some years later. I focused on the young founder of a group of liberal Catholic laity—Emmanuel Mounier of the Personalist Movement—and its seminal monthly review, *Esprit*. Ranging across the wide spectrum of Catholic opinion from Jacques Maritain to Gabriel Marcel, Mounier's review undertook, from 1932 till his death in 1951, the construction of a "third force" in politics that would transcend both socialism and capitalism. The critique of capitalism led a few Mounierians to a brief flirtation with the corporatist policies of Vichy. In the main, however, their sincerity was above reproach; and they appeared to be taken seriously in the immediate postwar era by the Mouvement Républicain Populaire, the ruling party in the Fourth Republic. But elevated ideals and careful theorizing were woefully inadequate to the exigencies of the Cold War, the fierce polarities between Left and Right, the disintegration of the empire, and the loss of national options in exchange for economic bailout under the Marshall Plan.

77

David Levering Lewis

When Mounier died suddenly, he had really run out of credible solutions to the raging crises of his time.[9]

A funny thing happened to me on the way to getting my Ph.D. Returning to London one night in late 1961 with about half of the dissertation to hand over to Pickles, I left my briefcase on the circle line tube. Two days later it still had not turned up in the lost and found. An English friend at LSE telephoned a public school chum of his who worked on a large-circulation daily. The next day a full column story about a hapless American's lost thesis ran alongside a full torso photograph of Brigitte Bardot in a swimsuit. For about a week I was a celebrity at the LSE. The two hundred typed pages of "Mounier" never turned up, alas. My tutor's consoling remark was that it would almost surely improve with a second version. With "Mounier" rewritten, defended, and accepted in the spring of 1962, I left England for Fort Benning, Georgia, and induction into the U.S. Army. By the time I got back to revising the dissertation for possible publication three years later, "Mounier" felt stale. I settled instead for a major article in the July 1970 issue of the *Catholic Historical Review*—"Emmanuel Mounier and the Politics of 'Moral Revolution': Aspects of Political Crisis in French Liberal Catholicism, 1935–38." Many of the judgments I made in that article have been sustained, I was pleased to see, in Tony Judt's recent book, *Past Imperfect: French Intellectuals, 1944–1956.*[10]

After basic training, the Army in its wisdom sent me right back to Europe in a special unit headquartered in a former SS complex on the German border with France. I got out of the army after eighteen months through an academic loophole that got me my first teaching post as a lecturer at the University of Ghana. I arrived in Accra two months after the death of W. E. B. Du Bois. I taught European Medieval and Renaissance history to some of the brightest students of my career to date and tried to remain neutral in the swirl of debate, rumor, and conspiracies in Nkrumah's Ghana. Assassination attempts against the president occurred just about

From Eurocentrism to Polycentrism

every other month—one or two of them probably financed by the CIA. Malcolm X passed through and left the sizeable African American community in a state of exaltation for weeks afterward. Professors were arrested, deported or, if Ghanaian, imprisoned. On one unforgettable occasion, when the "indignant socialist masses," as their carefully designed signs proclaimed, invaded the university demanding the expulsion of all expatriates, I found my American self standing smack in their line of march. "Where do you come from?" barked the leader of the socialist masses. When I gulped, "Atlanta," he shook my hand, saying, as he smiled broadly—"Welcome, to Ghana, brother." I left the University of Ghana with regret in 1964, after only one year.

At Howard, Notre Dame, and Morgan State College I taught the history and politics of the Third and Fourth French republics and some European survey courses. In the spring of 1968, after two research summers in Paris, I had begun to write the book that I hoped would establish my credentials in the field. It was to be called "The Clerc in Politics." It was a study of the ideas of eight French writers whose works had generated a dedicated public and political following—which included Mounier, Georges Bernanos, Louis Ferdinand Céline, Jean Guehenno, François Mauriac, and Pierre Drieu La Rochelle (no women, I'm now chagrinned to say). During the first week in March 1968, William Weatherby, formerly the *Manchester Guardian* correspondent to the United States and now a Penguin editor, wrote to me. Weatherby found out about me through our mutual friend Preston King. His letter proposed a biography of Martin Luther King, Jr.—part of Penguin's Great Leaders of the 20th Century series. I had already missed most of the civil rights revolution, had no professional interest in writing about it, and possessed only a vague impression of Martin Luther King, whom I'd seen briefly only twice—at Fisk in 1956, then again in 1958 at Bethel AME Church in Atlanta. Furthermore, it struck me as preposterous to write a biography of a thirty-nine-year-old, dynamic public figure. The book would probably be out of date before publication. Finally, although perhaps unintentionally, I suspected that Weatherby's proposal to an African American scholar trained in European history implied some special goodness of fit based on race that was demeaning. I was just about to mail my declination when the news broke on the evening of April 4 that Martin Luther King, Jr., had been shot to death in Memphis.

The rest, as they say, is history. King's assassination and the ensuing urban conflagrations turned what would have been a digression into a unique opportunity to write about the promise and the mirage of America as the land of opportunity. That summer, I blitzed the South, interviewing the principals; read the newspapers and the secondary publications; made the first use of the King papers at Boston University; tried mightily to persuade Mrs. Coretta Scott King to permit me to speak with her and to interview key Southern Christian Leadership Conference personalities. In deference to her wishes, many of Dr. King's intimates had pledged to remain silent until Mrs. King's large-advance book about her life with her husband, *My Life with Martin Luther King* (1969), was completed. For better or worse, I chose not to wait, finishing the research and writing the manuscript in nine months. Praeger published the hardcover edition in time for the second unofficial commemoration of Martin Luther King's birthday in January 1970. Its reception by professional historians was generally gratifying, with Louis Harlan calling it "an excellent book" in the *American Historical Review*. Unfortunately, I shot myself in the foot badly with the King family and much of the African American community by writing imprudently in the preface of my initial skepticism about Dr. King and by choosing for the biography's title—*King: A Critical Biography*. Bill Weatherby and I both overlooked the negative connotation of "critical" in American English. Mrs. King uttered a frosty appraisal. The Ministerial Alliance of Baltimore ordered parishioners not to read it—thereby making it a best-seller in Baltimore. Columbia's distinguished professor of government, Charles Hamilton, managed to write a politically correct review in the *Sunday Times Book Review* that said little about the biography and much about his own association with the Kings. Despite the curious treatment of what is now simply and safely, *King: a Biography*, it still enjoys an astonishing shelf life.[11]

But I still didn't get it—didn't fully awaken to the extraordinary abundance of virginal sources and the variety of germinal interpretations in African American historiography. Instead, I returned to French history, deferring work on "The Clerc in Politics" in order to write a potboiler of a research breakthrough on the Dreyfus Affair. With a decent advance from William Morrow & Company and royalties from *King*, I sailed away for a year in Europe with my former wife and two young children on a Yugoslavian freighter in summer 1971. The quest was to examine the so-called secret dossier on the Dreyfus case in the archives of the French military at Chateau de Vincennes. It had been examined once only by the chief of manuscripts of the Bibliothèque Nationale, Marcel Thomas, who lent his august influence to my petition to the authorities at Vincennes. The secret dossier consisted of evidence manufactured by Army intelligence against Dreyfus for the infamous second trial at Rennes. None of it had been used, however, because its fraudulence was finally deemed too obvious even for a military court martial. Rather than destroy the materials outright, the Army General Staff locked them away in 1899. When Monsieur Jean-Claude Devos, head of the Section Historique de l'Armée, turned the key in the lock on the metal cabinet in his office, I felt that day that the ultimate aphrodisiac is not power, but access to restricted documents.

The book, *Prisoners of Honor: The Dreyfus Affair*, was published in fall of 1973.[12] The Princeton reviewer in the *Times* was clearly perplexed that the African American biographer of Martin Luther King had written the book. The Oxford professor reviewing it for the *Washington Post*, Douglas Johnson, haughtily explained that I had gotten the story wrong: Anti-Semitism had played no part in Dreyfus's initial conviction. The *Los Angeles Times* liked the book a good deal better, as did the *St. Louis Post Dispatch*. By the time the Military Book Club of Great Britain took *Prisoners of Honor* as a main selection, I had already begun to reconsider my history agenda. Increasingly, I was known as King's principal biographer—inescapably so after publication of *Black Leaders of the Twentieth Century*, Franklin and Meier's 1982 edition containing my essay, "King and the Politics of Nonviolent Populism." The tug of African American history had grown stronger. Still, I resisted, partly out of loyalty to French history and to a Talented Tenth pride in defying stereotypes; partly out of aversion to what I regarded as the distortions stemming from bottom-up paradigms and overemphasis on slavery. I fully shared Kenneth Kusmer's astonishment that, as he would write later, "the attentions of historians of black America were riveted not on the origins and significance of the ghetto but on the institution of slavery."[13]

In 1976, I proposed a book to Knopf on the Harlem Renaissance. I hoped to write the first deeply researched, comprehensive study of that period. The fact that there were enormous collections of pertinent untouched correspondence at Howard's Moorland-Spingarn, the New York Public Library's Schomburg Center for Research in Black Culture, Fisk, Amistad (then at Dillard University in New Orleans), and the James Weldon Johnson Collection at the Beinecke Library at Yale made the topic another aphrodiasic of an experience. The five hundred boxes of Alain Locke letters at Howard alone would, I suspected, make for a sizzling reconstruction of Renaissance relationships. Beyond the zest for discovery and the relish of controversy, however, I had a larger agenda. It entailed taking up where August Meier and I had left off in that 1959 article on Atlanta in order to put class back into African American historiography. I was certain that these collections would tell me what I expected

From Eurocentrism to Polycentrism

to learn—that I would find clearly stated in these exchanges a self-conscious determination to construct an arts and letters movement in the service of civil rights advancement. *When Harlem Was in Vogue* appeared in 1980, and I believed I had proved my argument. I formulated it best in the preface to the book's third edition. "The Harlem Renaissance," I wrote, "reveals itself to be an elitist response on the part of a tiny group of mostly second-generation, college-educated, and generally affluent Afro-Americans—a response, first to the increasingly raw racism of the times, second, to the frightening Black Zionism of the Garveyites, and, finally, to the remote, but no less frightening appeal of Marxism."[14]

It was my advocacy of the paradigms of classism that prompted me to write one of my most misunderstood pieces. The Great Black Migration had sown a good deal of distress among established, genteel families of color in the North. The alien mores of the migrating farmers from the South, the increasing residential and workplace tensions caused by their influx, the utopian excesses of Garveyism—all of this put the black professional classes in Brooklyn, Philadelphia, and Chicago in fear of a northern white backlash that would wipe out the considerable civil rights gains they had slowly and carefully accumulated. I saw a parallel here with the response of German Jews to the problematic influx of Russian and east European Jews. I argued, therefore, that an alliance between affluent Jews and the Talented Tenth had come about in the NAACP and the National Urban League as a means of combatting a growing racism driven by the two migrations. "Parallels and Divergences: Assimilationist Strategies of Afro-American and Jewish Elites from 1910 to the Early Thirties" was published in the December 1984 *Journal of American History*.[15] Sadly, we have no control over those who hijack our ideas. But this does not make it one whit less dismaying and painful to have been simultaneously attacked as an anti-Semite and praised for being one. When the Jewish Museum of New York selected

David Levering Lewis

"Parallels and Divergences" as the lodestar piece in *Bridges and Boundaries: African Americans and American Jews*, the catalogue for its 1991 exhibition, I felt wonderfully vindicated.

Continuing to pursue paradigms of classism, I contributed the essay, "Origins and Causes of the Civil Rights Movement," to the 1986 University Press of Mississippi collection, *The Civil Rights Movement in America*. One of its insights was to underscore the lack of enthusiasm and even opposition by a portion of the South's African American professional classes to the NAACP's *Brown v. Board of Education* strategy. The end of segregated education meant the beginning of the end of the segregated black economy—a detail of social history that is only now being explored.[16] Five years later, in what many of my peers read as a querulous piece, I contributed the essay, "Radical History: Toward Inclusiveness," to a *Journal of American History* roundtable, "What Has Changed and Not Changed in American Historical Practice?" I argued that, notwithstanding frequent tributes paid to the liberating role of the civil rights revolution in the study of history, there was still much too much the tendency even among radical white historians to mine subjects such as slavery, segregation, migration, labor, and the urban crucible primarily to supply ammunition for arguments about mainstream history, instead of probing them for what they can tell us about the great complexity of African American life over time.

"The paradox of extolling the academic impact of a [social] movement while ignoring the academic voices within that movement raises a fundamental intellectual concern," I wrote, "for, although African American historiography has reached full adulthood, there remains an ambivalence about its place." That ambivalence derived from the assumption (subconscious) that the cardinal value of African American historiography was what it revealed about the classist, sexist, and economic hegemonies controlling the American past and present. It seemed to me that it was time, therefore, to begin writing the histories of people of color with far

From Eurocentrism to Polycentrism

greater emphasis upon the comparative and the integrative, rather than upon the separate, the different, and the parochial.[17] In other words, I suggested, in answer to the round-table question, that not that much had changed.

Gearing up to research the life and times of Du Bois, I found myself diverted again from African American history into a large experiment with comparative history. As with the Harlem Renaissance, the story here needed telling through a largely unmined lode of documents that revealed a largely unsuspected degree of strategizing and collaboration among late nineteenth-century Africans. Familiarity with the European archives and success in gaining access to the supposedly destroyed records of Marchand's Congo-Nile mission shed very different light on the Fashoda incident of 1898. The resulting book, *The Race to Fashoda: European Colonialism and African Resistance in the Scramble for Africa*, earned a gratifying kudo from the journal *Foreign Affairs*: "For the first time, a major history of the European colonial movement in Africa tells the story of the African resistance while also giving a parallel account of the European side."[18]

*W. E. B. Du Bois: Biography of a Race, 1868–1919* was published in October 1993, after eight years of research and writing. What began as a large, single-volume study became a two-volume enterprise, with the first book covering roughly the first half of the life and times of William Edward Burghardt Du Bois.[19] If it were ever desirable to try writing biography by committee, this was the subject to justify the effort. The density of material was a major consideration—110,000 items in the Du Bois correspondence alone, in addition to some eighty related archival collections, 200 pages of Freedom of Information Act releases, two hundred oral histories, several thousand miles of travel in West Africa, Eastern Europe, and the former Soviet Union, along with a continent of secondary reading matter, as well as thousands of pages of Du Bois editorials and book reviews, sixteen nonfiction monographs, and five novels.

85

David Levering Lewis

Always a controversial figure, Du Bois espoused racial and political beliefs of such variety and seeming contradiction as to bewilder and alienate as many Americans, black and white, as he inspired or converted. Beneath the shifting complexity of alliances and denunciations, nevertheless, there was a pattern, a congealing of inclinations, experiences, and ideas, more and more inclining Du Bois to a vision of society that became, in contrast to the lives of most men and women, increasingly radical as he grew older, until the day came when the civil liberties maverick was supplanted by the full-blown Marxist. That he was often arrogant and imprudent, maddeningly inconsistent, and even ultimately persuaded that treason was the last refuge of the true patriot are of less importance than that Du Bois's ideas were fecund and his obduracy deeply principled. I believed, as I embarked on the research for my Du Bois biography, that this was a subject of enormous significance. Mine has been, and will, therefore, continue to be until the completion of the second volume, an effort to appreciate a life that is the synecdoche of an epoch—a window onto virtually every salient issue of the twentieth century, from social science advocacy and civil rights to the politics of social democracy and anti-imperialism.

On that note, it is well to end this memoir. The review in *Foreign Affairs* expresses what my quest turns out largely to have been about—the unmasking of motives behind the complexity and similarity of individual and group interaction. The key to the quest turns out not to be French history, or U.S. history, or African American history, or African history. The quest is for histories. For me, the road has led from Eurocentrism to polycentrism. It means going beyond a given constellation of problems to other times, places, classes, and races in order to say something deeply informed about that which is unique, evolving, or sometimes just another variation of the age old gavotte of hegemony and resistance. It's an altogether exhilarating experience.

From Eurocentrism to Polycentrism

# NOTES

1. John Hope Franklin, "On the Evolution of Scholarship in Afro-American History," in Darlene Clark Hine, ed., *The State of Afro-American History: Past, Present, and Future* (Baton Rouge: Louisiana State University Press, 1986), p. 18.

2. Principal works by (and several about) first, second, and third generation scholars of African American history: George Washington Williams (1848–1891), *History of the Negro Race in America from 1619 to 1880* (New York: G. P. Putnam's Sons, 1882), 2 vols.; John Hope Franklin, *George Washington Williams: A Biography* (Chicago: University of Chicago Press, 1985); W. E. B. Du Bois (1868–1963), *The Suppression of the African Slave Trade to the United States of America, 1638–1870* (New York: Longman, Green, 1896); idem, *The Negro* (New York: Henry Holt, 1915); idem, *Black Reconstruction in America, 1860–1880* (New York: Harcourt, Brace, 1935); see also David Levering Lewis, *W. E. B. Du Bois: Biography of a Race, 1868–1919* (New York: John Macrae/Henry Holt, 1993); idem, "Introduction" to W. E. B. Du Bois, *Black Reconstruction in America: 1860–1880* (New York: Atheneum, 1992, orig. pub. 1935); Arnold Rampersad, *Art and Imagination of W. E. B. Du Bois* (Cambridge: Harvard University Press, 1976); Elliott Rudwick, *W. E. B. Du Bois: A Study in Minority Group Leadership* (Philadelphia: University of Pennsylvania Press, 1960); Carter G. Woodson (1875–1950), *The History of the Negro Church* (Washington, D.C.: Associated Publishers, 1921); idem, *Free Negro Owners of Slaves in the United States in 1830* (Washington, D.C.: Association for the Study of Negro Life and History, 1924); idem, *The Negro in Our History* (Washington, D.C.: Associated Publishers, 1927); see also Jacqueline Goggin, *Carter G. Woodson: A Life in Black History* (Baton Rouge: Louisiana State University Press, 1993); Charles H. Wesley (1891–1987), *Negro Labor in the United States, 1850–1925* (New York: Russell & Russell, orig. pub. 1927); idem, *Richard Allen: An Apostle of Freedom* (Washington, D.C.: Associated Publishers, 1935); Rayford W. Logan (1897–1982), *The Negro in American Life and Thought: The Nadir, 1877–1901* (New York: Dial Press, 1954); idem, *What the Negro Wants* (Chapel Hill: University of North Carolina Press, 1944); Kenneth R. Janken, *Rayford W. Logan and the Dilemma of the African-American Intellectual* (Amherst: University of Massachusetts Press, 1993); Helen G. Edmonds, *The Negro and Fusion Politics in North Carolina* (Chapel Hill: University of North Carolina Press, 1951); Benjamin Quarles, *Frederick Douglass* (Washington, D.C.: Associated Publishers, 1948); idem, *The Negro in the Civil War* (Boston: Little, Brown, 1953); idem, *Lincoln and the Negro* (New York: Oxford University Press, 1962); idem, *Black Abolitionists* (New York: Oxford Univer-

David Levering Lewis

sity Press, 1969); John Hope Franklin (1915–), *The Free Negro in North Carolina* (Chapel Hill: University of North Carolina Press, 1943); idem, *From Slavery to Freedom: A History of Negro Americans* (New York: Alfred A. Knopf, 1947); idem, *Reconstruction after the Civil War* (Chicago: University of Chicago Press, 1961); Herbert Aptheker, *Negro Slave Revolts in the United States, 1526–1860* (New York: International Publishers, 1939).

3. August Meier and Elliott Rudwick, *Black History and the Historical Profession, 1915–1980* (Urbana: University of Illinois Press, 1986), p. 179. David Levering Lewis (1936–), *King: A Critical Biography* (New York: Praeger, 1970). Selected works of fourth generation scholars of African American history: John Blassingame (1940–), *Black New Orleans, 1860–1880* (Chicago: University of Chicago Press, 1973); idem, *The Slave Community: Plantation Life in the Antebellum South* (New York: Oxford University Press, 1979); Nell I. Painter, *Exodusters: Black Migration to Kansas after Reconstruction* (Cambridge: Harvard University Press, 1976); Thomas C. Holt (1942–), *Black Over White: Negro Political Leadership in South Carolina during Reconstruction* (Urbana: University of Illinois Press, 1977); Nathan I. Huggins (1927–1987), *Harlem Renaissance* (New York: Oxford University Press, 1971); Eugene Genovese, *The Political Economy of Slavery* (New York: Pantheon, 1965); idem, *Roll, Jordan, Roll: The World the Slaves Made* (New York: Pantheon Books, 1974); Mary Frances Berry, *Black Resistance, White Law: A History of Constitutional Racism in America* (New York: Appleton-Century-Crofts, 1971); idem, *Military Necessity and Civil Rights Policy: Black Citizenship and the Constitution, 1861–1868* (Port Washington, N.Y.: Kennikat Press, 1977). Biographers of African American subjects: Stephen R. Fox, *The Guardian of Boston: William Monroe Trotter* (New York: Atheneum, 1970); Arnold Rampersad, op. cit., and *The Life of Langston Hughes* (New York: Oxford University Press, 1986–88), 2 vols.; Waldo E. Martin (1951–), *The Mind of Frederick Douglass* (Chapel Hill: University of North Carolina Press, 1984); Taylor Branch, *Parting the Waters: America in the King Years, 1954–63* (New York: Simon and Schuster, 1988); Kenneth R. Manning, *Black Apollo of Science: The Life of Ernest Everett Just* (New York: Oxford University Press, 1983); Wilson J. Moses, *Alexander Crummell: A Study of Civilization and Discontent* (New York: Oxford University Press, 1989); Dickson D. Bruce, Jr., *Archibald Grimke: Portrait of a Black Independent* (Baton Rouge: Louisiana State University Press, 1993).

4. W. E. B. Du Bois, "Little Rock," *Chicago Defender*, June 14, 1947, cited in Herbert Aptheker, ed., *Newspaper Columns by W. E. B. Du Bois* (White Plains, N.Y.: Kraus-Thomson Organization, 1986), p. 717.

5. Willard B. Gatewood, *Aristocrats of Color: The Black Elite, 1880–1920* (Bloomington: Indiana University Press, 1990), p. 343.

6. The Fisk University faculty was exceptionally well endowed. Edward Pessen would publish his first book shortly after leaving Fisk,

From Eurocentrism to Polycentrism

Most Uncommon Jacksonians: The Radical Leaders of the Early Labor Movement (Albany: State University of New York Press, 1967). Robert Hayden would migrate to the University of Michigan and achieve the distinction, shortly before his early death, of becoming poetry consultant at the Library of Congress (now upgraded to Poet Laureate of the United States); see Hayden, *Words in the Mourning Time: Poems* (New York: October House, 1970). David Granick's *Red Executive: Study of the Organization Man in Russian Industry* (Garden City: Doubleday, 1960). August Meier completed the revisions for the Columbia dissertation published as *Negro Thought in America: 1880–1915* (Ann Arbor: University of Michigan, 1963), now a classic. Bernard Spivack's *Shakespeare and the Allegory of Evil* was published by Columbia University Press in 1958. Aaron Douglas continued to paint during his years as professor of art and art history.

7. August Meier and David Levering Lewis, "History of the Negro Upper Class in Atlanta, Georgia, 1890–1950," *Journal of Negro Education* (Spring 1959): 128–39.

8. Preston T. King, *Fear of Power* (London: Frank Cass, 1967); see also *The Ideology of Order: A Comparative Analysis of Jean Bodin and Thomas Hobbes* (New York: Barnes & Noble, 1974).

9. See John Hellman, *Emmanuel Mounier and the New Catholic Left, 1930–1950* (Toronto: University of Toronto Press, 1981); Tony Judt, *Past Imperfect: French Intellectuals, 1944–1956* (Berkeley: University of California Press, 1992), esp. pp. 140–42, 304–305, and passim; and Rufus William Rauch, *Politics and Belief in Contemporary France: Emmanuel Mounier and Christian Democracy, 1932–1950* (The Hague: M. Nijhoff, 1972).

10. David Levering Lewis, "Emmanuel Mounier and the Politics of 'Moral Revolution': Aspects of Political Crisis in French Liberal Catholicism, 1935–38," *Catholic Historical Review* 56 (July 1970): 266–90; Judt, *Past Imperfect*, pp. 86–90.

11. David Levering Lewis, *King: A Critical Biography* (New York: Praeger, 1970; Urbana: University of Illinois Press, 1978).

12. David Levering Lewis, *Prisoners of Honor: The Dreyfus Affair* (New York: William Morrow & Company, 1973). The definitive work remains Marcel Thomas's *L'Affaire sans Dreyfus* (Paris: A. Fayard, 1961).

13. Kenneth L. Kusmer, "The Black Urban Experience in American History," in Hine, ed., *State of Afro-American History*, p. 96.

14. David Levering Lewis, *When Harlem Was in Vogue* (New York: Oxford University Press, 1989), p. xvi.

15. David Levering Lewis, "Parallels and Divergences: Assimilationist Strategies of Afro-American and Jewish Elites from 1910 to the Early Thirties," *Journal of American History* 71 (December 1984): 543–64; republished under the same title in J. Salzman, ed., *Bridges and Boundaries: African*

David Levering Lewis

*Americans and American Jews* (New York: Braziller/Jewish Museum, 1992), pp. 17–35.

16. David Levering Lewis, "The Origins and Causes of the Civil Rights Movement," in Charles W. Eagles, ed., *The Civil Rights Movement in America* (Oxford: University of Mississippi Press, 1984), pp. 83–97.

17. David Levering Lewis, "Radical History: Toward Inclusiveness," *Journal of American History* 76 (September 1989): 471–74.

18. David Levering Lewis, *The Race to Fashoda: European Colonialism and African Resistance in the Scramble for Africa* (New York: Weidenfeld & Nicolson, 1988); idem, "The Race to Fashoda," *Foreign Affairs* (Summer 1988).

19. David Levering Lewis, *W. E. B. Du Bois: Biography of a Race, 1868–1919* (New York: Henry Holt and Company, 1993).

From Eurocentrism to Polycentrism

# 6. My Life as a Historian

Eric Foner is DeWitt Clinton Professor of History at Columbia University. He earned a bachelor's degree at Columbia in 1963 and another at Oriel College, Oxford
University, in 1965. He completed his doctorate at Columbia in 1969. Professor Foner has also taught at City
College and the Graduate Center of the City University of
New York and has held appointments as Pitt Professor of
American History and Institutions at Cambridge University, Fulbright Professor of American History at Moscow
State University, and Harmsworth Professor of American History at Oxford University. He has held fellowships
from the American Council of Learned Societies, the Guggenheim Foundation, and the National Endowment for the
Humanities, and in 1989 he was elected to the American Academy of Arts and Sciences. He also served as president of the Organization of American Historians in
1993–94. Professor Foner's many publications include
Free Soil, Free Labor, Free Men: The Ideology
of the Republican Party Before the Civil War
(1970, 1995), Tom Paine and Revolutionary
America (1976), and Politics and Ideology in
the Age of the Civil War (1980). Nothing but
Freedom: Emancipation and Its Legacy (1983)
was originally presented as the Walter Lynwood Fleming
Lectures at Louisiana State University. His Reconstruc-

tion: America's Unfinished Revolution, 1863–
1877 won the Bancroft Prize in American History, the
Parkman Prize, and the Owsley Prize, among others. He
also won acclaim for his work as curator of the Chicago
Historical Society's A House Divided exhibit. Professor
Foner is currently completing a history of the concept of
freedom in America.

Historians, by and large, are not noted for introspection.
Our calling requires us to analyze past events, but we rarely
turn our interpretive talents upon ourselves. I welcome this
opportunity to reflect publicly about how and why I became
a historian, how my approach to the study of history has
changed over time, and how the concerns of the present
have helped to shape the questions I ask about the past.

Born in New York City in 1943, I was raised in Long
Beach, Long Island, to all outward appearances a typical
child of America's postwar suburban boom. In one respect,
however, my upbringing was unusual, although emblem-
atic, nonetheless, of one aspect of the American experience.
Shortly before I was born, my father, Jack D. Foner, and my
uncle, Philip S. Foner, both historians at City College, were
among some sixty faculty members dismissed from teaching positions at the City University after informers named
them as members of the Communist party. A few years later,
my mother was forced to resign from her job as a high
school art teacher. During my childhood and for many years
afterward, my parents were blacklisted and unable to teach.
Unlike most of my generation, I did not have to wait until
the upheavals of the 1960s to discover the yawning gap that
separated America's professed ideals and its self-confident
claim to be a land of liberty, from its social and political
reality. My friend Gabor Boritt, who grew up in communist
Hungary and now directs the Civil War Institute at Gettys-
burg College, once remarked to me, "I was raised in a country where we understood that most of what the government

says is untrue." "That's funny," I replied, "I grew up in the same country."

Given the profession of my father and uncle, it seems in retrospect inevitable that I would become a historian. But, as I frequently tell my students, events are inevitable only after they happen. As a youth I wanted to be an astronomer, and my first published book was entitled *The Solar System*. To be sure, "published" is a bit of an exaggeration. The book, with one chapter on each planet, was dictated by me, typed by my mother, and illustrated by a family friend. It was not based on archival research. But I was only seven years old at the time.

My greatest joy as a youth was gazing through a telescope on spring nights, and my idea of athletic prowess was serving on the Long Beach High School math team (we finished second in Long Island one year). But I also imbibed a lively interest in both history and current events. Historical and political concerns suffused our household. Every child thinks his upbringing is entirely normal. Only gradually did I realize that other families did not discuss the intricacies of international relations and domestic politics over the dinner table, or follow election returns in France, India, and Guatemala as avidly as those in the United States.

What was truly distinctive about my family's view of both American history and the world around us, however, was our preoccupation with the past and present condition of our black fellow countrymen. As suburbs go, Long Beach was a liberal community, whose predominantly Jewish residents regularly voted Democratic. But on issues relating to race, the prevailing sentiment was indifference. Our idyllic town had its own small ghetto, home to black domestic servants, but no one except my parents and a few like-minded friends seemed aware of its existence, or wondered why housing there was so inferior to that enjoyed by whites. In school, we did commemorate Negro History Week, mostly with lessons about George Washington Carver and his amazing feats with peanuts. But our history texts were typi-

Eric Foner

cal of the time—slavery, they taught, was a regrettable but not particularly oppressive institution, Reconstruction a terrible mistake, and blacks played no discernible role whatever in the rest of American history. I well recall my mother (to my embarrassment), striding into school to complain about the illustrations of happy slaves playing banjos in our third-grade history text. The principal could not understand her unhappiness. "What difference does it make," he asked, "what we teach them about slavery?"

In my home, however, it made a great deal of difference. As the work of Mark Naison and other scholars has shown, in the 1930s the Communist Party was the only predominantly white organization to make fighting racism central to its political program. Communist-oriented historians such as Herbert Aptheker and my uncle, Philip Foner, along with black scholars such as W. E. B. Du Bois, had begun the process of challenging prevailing stereotypes about black history. At home, I learned ideas today taken for granted but then virtually unknown outside black and left-wing circles: Slavery was the fundamental cause of the Civil War and emancipation its greatest accomplishment; Reconstruction was a tragedy not because it was attempted but because it failed; the condition of blacks was the nation's foremost domestic problem. Du Bois and Paul Robeson were friends of my family, Frederick Douglass (whom my uncle had rescued from historical oblivion by publishing a four-volume collection of his magnificent writings and speeches) a household name. In my home we followed with a growing sense of excitement the unfolding of the civil rights movement, and it was assumed that my younger brother and I would participate in it. Tom went on to take part in the Mississippi Freedom Summer of 1964. I not only attended the March on Washington of 1963 but also the less well-known March of 1957; and in 1960 I spent a great deal of time picketing Woolworth stores in New York in support of the Southern sit-ins. By then, I was a freshman at Columbia College,

*My Life as a Historian*

where during my undergraduate years I became the first president of ACTION, a student political party that, along with sponsoring folk music concerts, issued newsletters on civil rights and persuaded the off-campus housing registry to drop listings by landlords who would not sign a nondiscrimination pledge.

I entered Columbia fully intending to major in astronomy. By the end of my sophomore year my interest—or perhaps my talent—in science had waned considerably. Then, in my junior year, I somehow persuaded James P. Shenton to allow me to enroll in his senior seminar on the Civil War period. By the end of the year, I was not only a history major but had developed what has become a lifelong passion for that era.

Looking back over my career, I realize that I learned from two great teachers what it is to be a historian. The first was my father. Deprived of his livelihood while I was growing up, he supported our family as a freelance lecturer on history and current affairs. Listening to his lectures, I came to appreciate how present concerns can be illuminated by the study of the past—how the repression of the McCarthy era recalled the days of the Alien and Sedition Acts, how the civil rights movement needed to be viewed in light of the great struggles of black and white abolitionists, and how in the brutal suppression of the Philippine insurrection at the turn of the century could be found the antecedents of American intervention in Iran, Guatemala, and Vietnam. I also imbibed a way of thinking about the past in which visionaries and underdogs—Tom Paine, Wendell Phillips, Eugene V. Debs, and W. E. B. Du Bois—were as central to the historical drama as presidents and captains of industry, and how a commitment to social justice could infuse one's attitudes toward the past. The second great teacher was Jim Shenton, legendary at Columbia for his dramatic lecturing style and the personal interest he took in his students—down to introducing us to the city's culinary attractions.

Eric Foner

From Shenton I learned that successful teaching rests on both a genuine and selfless concern for students and the ability to convey to them a love of history.

My seminar paper that year was a study of the Free Soil Party of 1848, a justifiably obscure topic that led to my first excursion into archival research, in my senior thesis, supervised by Richard Hofstadter. The fact that the civil rights movement was then reaching its crescendo powerfully affected my choice of subject—the racial attitudes of those who opposed the expansion of slavery. Just two years earlier, Leon F. Litwack had stunned the historical profession with his demonstration, in North of Slavery, that racism was every bit as pervasive in the antebellum North as the slave-holding South. My research built on his insight in order to demonstrate that many free soilers opposed the expansion of slavery in order to keep blacks, free or slave, from competing with "free white labor."

My senior thesis became the basis of my first two published articles, which appeared in 1965. More importantly, it introduced me to Hofstadter, the premier historian of his generation, who would soon be supervising my dissertation. There was a certain irony in our relationship. Back in 1941, Hofstadter had obtained his first full-time teaching position at the downtown branch of City College, when a position had opened because of the dismissal of my father. Whatever thoughts he harbored about this twist of fate, Hofstadter played brilliantly the role of intellectual mentor so crucial to any student's career. His books directed me toward the subjects that have defined much of my own writing—the history of political ideologies and the interconnections between social development and political culture.

Years later I learned that it was thanks to Hofstadter that on graduating from college, I was awarded a Kellett Fellowship to study at Oriel College, Oxford. The tutorial system, in which the student prepares a paper each week and reads

*My Life as a Historian*

it aloud to the tutor, gave me invaluable training in quick, clear expository writing. Each week, I was forced to master a subject about which I previously knew nothing—the reasons for the decline of the medieval wool trade, for example—and to present my ideas in a coherent fashion. I probably owe it to my years in Oxford that writers' block has never been one of my problems. At the end of my stay, I decided to return to Columbia to pursue a doctorate in American history. My decision was not greeted with universal enthusiasm. When I told my tutor, W. A. Pantin, a specialist on the English church in the fourteenth century, that I wanted to devote my career to the American past, he replied: "In other words, you have ceased to study history."

I returned to Columbia in 1965. While I was away, the sixties had happened. Students now wore long hair, colorful attire, and spent much of their time imbibing substances of questionable legality. Vietnam had replaced race as the predominant issue on campus; it would soon become the catalyst for a full-scale generational rebellion. Like so many others, I threw myself into the antiwar movement, but intellectually, I remained preoccupied with issues surrounding slavery and race, a preoccupation that deepened between 1965 and 1968 as America's cities burned, the civil rights movement evaporated, and it became clear that racism was far more deeply entrenched in American life than we had imagined a few short years before.

Somehow, while participating in events from antiwar marches to the Columbia student rebellion of 1968, I managed to write my dissertation, which became the basis of my first book, *Free Soil, Free Labor, Free Men*. A study of the ideology of the Republican party before the Civil War, the dissertation grew out of my old interest in free soilism. Among my aims was to outline Republicans' complex attitudes toward blacks, but I was deeply impressed by a comment by Winthrop Jordan at a conference I attended in 1966: "To understand people's attitudes about race, you have to understand their attitudes about everything." Jordan's remark helped me conceptualize my theme as a study of ideology—the coherent world view that brought together reinforcing attitudes about labor, economic growth, westward expansion, and race relations, and which inspired Republicans to oppose slavery's expansion and the growth of Southern political power. Published in 1970, my book became part of a trend whereby American historians rediscovered the value of the concept of ideology. Events of the time strongly influenced this development. In a society engulfed by social crisis, it no longer seemed plausible to argue, with 1950s "consensus" historians, that Americans had never disagreed profoundly over social and political issues.

Looking back from the vantage point of twenty-five years, *Free Soil* seems a curiously old-fashioned book. Written, as it were, on the threshold separating two generations of historical scholarship, it lacked the benefit of the "new histories" that have matured since 1970 and have focused historians' attention on the experiences of ordinary men and women rather than political leaders. History education at Columbia in those days resolutely favored the political and intellectual. But when I returned to England for the 1972–73 academic year to pursue work for my next project, a history of American radicalism, I encountered the new social and labor history. My historical writing would never be the same. Today, when we take for granted that history must include the experience of previously neglected groups—blacks, women, laborers, and others—it is difficult to recapture the sense of intellectual excitement produced by the works of E. P. Thompson, Eric Hobsbawm, and other British practitioners of "history from below." Thanks to what came to be called the "new social history," which they inspired, we today have a far more complex and nuanced portrait of the American past in all its diversity and contentiousness.

98

Of course, the inclusion of these diverse experiences in teaching and writing is not without its difficulties, as I had already discovered. In 1969, I was offered a job as an instructor in history at Columbia. As the department's junior member, I soon found myself sitting as an outside examiner on doctoral dissertations from other departments, with fascinating subjects such as "Tree Imagery in Emerson" and "The Belgian Press and the Boer War." But the main reason I was hired was to teach Columbia's first course in Afro-American history. My qualifications lay in a course on the subject I had offered in Double Discovery, a summer program for minority high school students, and my writings on free soil and race. Inevitably and understandably, many of Columbia's black students felt that the first such course offered in the College's 200-year history ought to be offered by a black scholar. But I was eager to teach the course, and insisted—as I continue to believe—that teaching and writing in black history should be held to the same standards as in any other academic discipline. The race of the instructor is not among them.

At any rate, I prepared avidly for the course, reading everything I could get my hands on, and for the first few weeks my expertise disarmed my critics. But a month into the term a group of black students began demonstrating both in and out of class, denouncing the course, in the idiom of the day, as a racist insult (although, as they told me privately, they actually liked my lectures and had nothing "personal" against me). For the rest of the term there were walkouts and disruptions, although most of the 150 students in the class attended every lecture and seemed eager to hear me teach the subject. After this baptism by fire, nothing that has happened in a classroom has ever fazed me. Out of that course came my next two publications: *America's Black Past*, an anthology of writings in the field, and *Nat Turner*, a documentary collection about America's greatest slave rebel. Since 1969, I have taught black history many

Eric Foner

times with little problem. Equally importantly, over the years I have fully integrated the black experience into my general courses on nineteenth-century history.

My initial career at Columbia lasted only three years. While I was in England, the department informed me that I should not expect to receive tenure. I was bitterly disappointed, but this rebuff turned out to be an immense stroke of good fortune. City College had just hired Herbert Gutman to revitalize its history department, and Herb offered me a job. So in 1973 I moved to a college one mile uptown from Columbia but as remote from it in other ways as if it were located on the far side of the moon. City was in the throes of adjusting to open admissions, with a faculty bitterly divided against itself. At my first department meeting, one colleague called another "a perjured slanderer," whereupon the second launched a lawsuit for defamation of character. But coming to City was the best thing that had ever happened to me, as both a teacher and a historian. It brought me into contact with an entirely different group of students—the children of the city's white ethnic, black, and Hispanic working class, nearly all of them the first members of their families to attend college. Some were woefully unprepared, others quite ready to take advantage of the opportunity that had suddenly been opened to them. Life at City was by turns inspiring and frustrating, but I have no doubt that the challenge made me a much better teacher.

Equally remarkable was the intellectual community Gutman had assembled, including brilliant young American historians such as Leon Fink, Virginia Yans, and Eric Perkins. At the center of the group stood Gutman himself, with his irrepressible enthusiasm for recovering the history of forgotten Americans, from coal miners and silk workers in Gilded Age America, to slaves. Under his influence, my education as a historian continued apace. My second book, *Tom Paine and Revolutionary America*, was powerfully influenced both by my recent stay in England and by Gutman's work. Like *Free Soil*, this was essentially a study of political ideology, but

My Life as a Historian

now I grounded Paine's writings firmly in the social history of his diverse environments, especially lower-class London and Philadelphia, and explored the role of social movements, not just political parties, in the dissemination of political ideas.

Having completed *Tom Paine*, I prepared to return to my long-delayed history of American radicalism. (Paine was supposed to have been the first chapter, but when I sat down to write it, the chapter had come to over 200 pages, a book in its own right.) But fate, in the person of Richard Morris, intervened. Totally unexpectedly, Morris invited me to write the volume on Reconstruction for the New American Nation series, of which he and Henry Steele Commager were editors. Although I had written nothing on Reconstruction except for an essay on Thaddeus Stevens (another prospective chapter in my ill-fated radicalism book), I had long had an interest in this, the most controversial and misunderstood period in all of American history.

Years before I had presented my own interpretation of Reconstruction to my ninth grade American history class at Long Beach high school. Our teacher was Mrs. Bertha Berryman, affectionately known among the students as Big Bertha (after a famous piece of World War I artillery). Following the then-dominant view of the era, Mrs. Berryman described the Reconstruction Act of 1867, which gave the right to vote to black men in the South, as the worst law in all of American history. I raised my hand and proposed that the Alien and Sedition Acts were "worse." Whereupon Mrs. Berryman replied, "If you don't like the way I'm teaching, Eric, why don't you come in tomorrow and give your own lesson on Reconstruction?" This I proceeded to do, admittedly with my father's help, in a presentation based largely on W. E. B. Du Bois's portrait of Reconstruction as a pivotal moment in the struggle for democracy in America. At the end of the class, Mrs. Berryman, herself a true democrat, announced: "Class, you have heard me, and you have heard Eric. Now let us vote to see who was right." I wish I could

Eric Foner

report that my persuasive presentation carried the day. In fact, only one student voted for me, my intrepid friend Neil Kleinman.

It therefore seemed almost preordained—like something out the life of Shirley MacLaine—when Morris offered me the chance to get even with Mrs. Berryman. I soon discovered that I had agreed to take on a project with a checkered past. In 1948, Howard K. Beale had agreed to do the book; he died eleven years later without having written a word. He was succeeded by David Donald. In 1969, Donald published an article lamenting that he had found it impossible to synthesize in a single account the political, economic, social, and intellectual developments of the era, and the course of national, Northern, and Southern events. The effort to do so seemed to make him despair of the entire enterprise of chronicling the nation's past. He had come to the conclusion, Donald wrote, that "the United States does not have a history." In 1975 he abandoned the project to devote himself to a more manageable one, a biography of Thomas Wolfe.

Fools, they say, rush in where angels fear to tread. I assumed I could do a year or two of reading and complete the book soon afterward. In fact, it took about ten years to research and write it. The turning point in my conceptualization of the project came in 1978, when I was invited to teach for a semester at the University of South Carolina in Columbia. There, in the State Archives, I encountered 121 thickly packed boxes of correspondence received by the state's Reconstruction governors. The letters contained an incredibly rich record, largely untapped by scholars, of local social and political life in the state. Before my eyes unfolded tales of utopian hopes and shattered dreams, of struggles for human dignity and ignoble violence by the Ku Klux Klan, of racism and black-white cooperation, of how everyday life had become "politicized" in ways barely hinted at in the existing literature. I realized that to tell the story of Reconstruction I could not rely on available scholarship, impres-

*My Life as a Historian*

sive as much of it was, but would have to delve into the archives to recover the local texture of life. In ensuing years, my research introduced me to an amazing cast of characters—former slaves seeking to breathe substantive meaning into the freedom they had acquired, up-country farmers struggling to throw off the heritage of racism, planters seeking to retain control of their now emancipated labor force, and Klansmen seeking to subvert the far-reaching changes of the era. Like Du Bois half a century earlier, I became convinced that the freedpeople were the central actors in the drama of Reconstruction. Rather than simply victims of manipulation or passive recipients of the actions of others, they were agents of change whose demand for individual and community autonomy helped to establish the agenda of Reconstruction politics.

Another unexpected development also affected the project's conceptualization. For the 1980–81 academic year, I was invited to teach as the Pitt Professor of American History at Cambridge University. Once again, a stay in England broadened my horizons as a historian. Prompted by some of my colleagues, I began to read about the aftermath of slavery in the British Empire, especially the Caribbean and South Africa. I soon discovered that this literature, much of it virtually unknown to scholars of American history, approached the transition from slavery to freedom in rather different ways than our own historical literature. Instead of defining the problem primarily as one of race relations, the predominant view in this country, scholars in Britain, Africa, and the Caribbean focused attention on the labor question after slavery—how former slaves struggled to secure economic autonomy while former planters, often aided by the British government, sought to encourage them to return to work on the plantations and, when unsuccessful, imported indentured laborers from China and India to take their place. The same issues of access to economic resources and control of labor, I became convinced, were central to the aftermath of slavery in the Reconstruction South. But

Eric Foner

my reading also underscored for me the uniqueness of Reconstruction, for only in this country were former slaves, within a few years of emancipation, given the right to vote and only here did they exercise a significant degree of political power on the state and local levels. Historians at that time were prone to describe Reconstruction as essentially conservative since it adhered to constitutional forms and did not distribute land to the former slaves. I became convinced that enfranchising the freedmen constituted, both in a comparative perspective and in the context of the racism of antebellum America, a truly radical experiment in interracial democracy.

In 1982, I returned to Columbia to teach, and here, over the next few years, the book was written. There is a certain irony in the fact that a Columbia historian produced this new history of Reconstruction, exemplified by the fact that my research expenses were partly covered by the department's Dunning Fund and much of my reading took place in Burgess Library. For it was at Columbia at the turn of the century that William A. Dunning and John W. Burgess had established the traditional school of Reconstruction scholarship, teaching that blacks were "children" incapable of appreciating the freedom that had been thrust upon them and that the North did a "monstrous thing" in granting them suffrage. There is no better illustration than Reconstruction of how historical interpretation both reflects and helps to shape current policies. The views of the Dunning School helped freeze the white South for generations in unalterable opposition to any change in race relations and justified decades of Northern indifference to Southern nullification of the 14th and 15th Amendments. The civil rights revolution, in turn, produced an outpouring of revisionist literature, far more favorable to the aspirations of the former slaves.

I think it was the historian C. Vann Woodward who first called the civil rights movement the Second Reconstruction. Although history never really repeats itself, the parallels be-

*My Life as a Historian*

tween the period after the Civil War and the 1950s and 1960s are very dramatic, as are the retreats from the Reconstruction ideal of racial justice and social equality in the latter decades of the nineteenth century and again in our own time. The issues that agitate race relations today—affirmative action, the role of the federal government in enforcing the rights of citizens, the possibility of interracial political coalitions, the relationship between economic and political equality—were also central to the debates of Reconstruction. Most strikingly, perhaps, both Reconstructions failed adequately to address the economic plight of black America, itself the legacy of 250 years of slavery and a century of segregation. The first Reconstruction did not respond to the former slaves' thirst for land. The second, which gave rise to a large black middle class, left millions of blacks trapped in decaying urban centers and deindustrializing sectors of the economy. Like the Reconstruction generation, we have seen radical movements rise to prominence, then retreat and shatter. Like them we have seen the resurgence of ideologies of social Darwinism, biological inferiority, and states rights that blame the victims of discrimination for their plight or insist that the federal government must not interfere with local traditions of inequality. Just as the failure of the first Reconstruction left to future generations an unfinished agenda of racial and social justice, the waning of the second has shown how far America still has to go in living up to the ideal of equality.

Published in 1988, my book on Reconstruction received a gratifying response—it won several prizes from historical organizations, was a finalist for the National Book Award, and sold far more copies than I was accustomed to. Reviewers praised its voluminous research and the way I integrated the era's numerous themes into a coherent whole. But ultimately, the book's merits derive from the fact that I care deeply about the issues of racial justice central to Reconstruction and to our society today. If *Reconstruction* was born in the archives, it was written from the heart.

Eric Foner

With the publication of *Reconstruction*, I assumed I would turn my scholarly attention to other areas. But things have not turned out this way. In the course of my research, I had gathered an immense file of biographical information about black political leaders in the postwar South—justices of the peace, sheriffs, and state legislators, as well as Congressmen and U.S. Senators—most of them unknown even to scholars. I brought this information together in *Freedom's Lawmakers*, a directory containing capsule biographies of nearly 1,500 individuals. My hope was to put these men, as it were, on the map of history, to make available the basic data concerning their lives and to bury irrevocably such misconceptions as that Reconstruction's leaders were illiterate, propertyless, and incompetent.

As *Freedom's Lawmakers* indicates, I seem unable to escape the Reconstruction era. I am currently the historical advisor for a projected television documentary on the period and curator of a museum exhibition—the first ever to be devoted exclusively to the period—that opened in 1996 at the Virginia Historical Society in Richmond. This latter project emerged from another unexpected twist in my career, my emergence as something of a public historian.

Shortly before I finished my book on Reconstruction, I was asked by the Chicago Historical Society to develop, along with one of their curators, Olivia Mahoney, a major exhibition on the Civil War era. My initial response was that they had approached the wrong person. I have no background in the study of material culture or in museum work. As a teacher, I am resolutely old-fashioned—I never use slides, films, or other audio-visual aids, except for a tattered map of the United States that I began tacking to the classroom wall after discovering that students in New York City do not know the location of the Mississippi River. But, the society's directors assured me, they had plenty of staff who could design exhibitions. What they needed was up-to-date historical thinking. For years, one of their most popular rooms had been the Lincoln Gallery, a collection of memorabilia such as the Great Emancipator's top hat, a piece of wood from his log cabin, some photos, and dioramas of scenes, real and mythic, from his life. The exhibition was popular, but it was not history. The society proposed to replace it with a full-scale account of the causes and conduct of the Civil War. As curator, my job was to outline the major historical themes, write labels, and, working with Mahoney, choose the objects to be included in the show. The only stipulation was that the exhibit had to include the bed on which Lincoln died after having been shot at Ford's Theater. This had somehow come into the society's possession and people traveled from far and wide to see it. Otherwise, I had complete intellectual freedom—I could do and say pretty much anything I wanted.

Like other historians, I have often lamented that scholars too often speak only to themselves and seem to have abandoned the effort to address a broader public. How could I refuse this invitation to help shape how hundreds of thousands of visitors who may never have attended a university history class or read an academic treatise understand a pivotal era of our country's history? So I accepted, thus embarking on what became, for me, a thoroughly enjoyable process of learning by doing. The finished exhibit, *A House Divided: America in the Age of Lincoln*, is unabashedly interpretive. It explores the contrast between free and slave labor and the societies built upon them, focuses on slavery as the primary cause of the Civil War, devotes attention to both abolitionism and Northern racism, and along with accounts of the military history of the war also stresses the process of emancipation as central to the war's meaning. Lincoln is present, but as a figure located firmly within his own time, not as an icon standing outside it. The exhibit has been a great success, not only winning several awards but inspiring other museums to bring in historians to upgrade outdated presentations of history.

Eric Foner

My new role in public history has involved me in a realm suddenly filled with controversy—witness the evisceration of the Smithsonian Museum's proposed exhibition on the dropping of the first atomic bomb, or the Library of Congress canceling a small show on the life and material surroundings of slaves. Of course, vigorous debate about how history should be studied and taught is healthy and inevitable in a democratic society. But too often, critics of innovative exhibitions—whether veterans' groups in the case of the Smithsonian, or black employees of the Library of Congress—reveal a desire for a history that eliminates complexity from our national experience, and a discomfort with the act of historical interpretation itself, as if fact and interpretation could somehow be hermetically sealed off from one another. I am eagerly looking forward to the reaction to the Richmond Reconstruction exhibit, which is as overtly interpretative as the Chicago show, and will, I hope, force at least some visitors to consider that much of what they thought they knew about the period is wrong.

Only recently have my scholarly interests moved on from Reconstruction. Currently, I am at work on a book, tentatively entitled *The Story of American Freedom*, which will trace how various Americans have interpreted and defined freedom, so central an element of our national consciousness, from the Revolution to the present. The book will build on my earlier writings on free labor, emancipation, and Reconstruction, but unlike my previous work, will bring me into the twentieth century. My theme is that rather than a fixed category or predetermined concept, freedom has always been a terrain of struggle. Its definition has been constantly created and recreated, its meanings constructed not only in Congressional debates and political treatises, but on plantations and picket lines, in parlors and bedrooms. It has been invoked by those in power to legitimate their aims, and seized upon by others seeking to transform society. In our own time, we have seen the putative division of the planet

*My Life as a Historian*

into free and nonfree worlds invoked by our government to justify violations of individual liberties at home and support for some highly repressive governments abroad. Yet within my lifetime, as well, the greatest mass movement of the century reinvigorated the language of freedom with its freedom rides, freedom songs, and the insistent cry, Freedom Now. The story of American freedom, in other words, is as contentious, as multidimensional, as American society itself.

Let me close, however, not by looking forward to a book still in its embryonic stage, but back two years, when I again spent the academic year in England, this time as Harmsworth Professor of American History at Oxford. Once again, living there seemed to expand my intellectual horizons, bringing me into contact, just as I was embarking on my study of freedom, with social historians of language and historians of political thought. But the year's highlight came not in England but five thousand miles to the south. That summer I was invited to lecture in South Africa, shortly after it had experienced its first democratic elections. As a historian of Reconstruction, the photographs, broadcast around the world, of men and women waiting in endless lines to cast their first ballots, brought to mind the scenes of celebration in our own country when former slaves voted for the first time after the Civil War. It was a reminder, in these days of cynicism about politics and democracy, that voting can be a deeply empowering act.

On the day before I left South Africa, I delivered the T. B. Davie Memorial Lecture at the University of Cape Town, named in honor of a vice chancellor who courageously defended academic freedom during the 1950s. Thirty-five years earlier, when the government imposed apartheid on South African universities, students had marched to the Parliament to extinguish a torch of freedom. After my lecture, the torch was relit to symbolize the birth of a new South Africa. It was a moment of genuine emotion, illus-

Eric Foner

trating the interconnectedness of past, present, and future. It seemed to me fitting that a historian was chosen to speak at this occasion, and an honor to be the one, especially since I know from my own upbringing how fragile freedom can be.

# 7. Autobiography and Scholarship

Jacqueline Jones is Truman Professor of American Civilization at Brandeis University. She earned her B.A. in American Studies at the University of Delaware in 1970 and went on to do graduate work in history at the University of Wisconsin, Madison, where she received her M.A. in 1972 and her Ph.D. in 1976. Professor Jones taught at Wellesley College and was Clare Boothe Luce Visiting Professor of History at Brown University before assuming her chair at Brandeis in 1991. She has held numerous fellowships, including two from the American Council of Learned Societies. Among her many publications are Soldiers of Light and Love: Northern Teachers and Georgia Blacks, 1865–1873 (1980) and The Dispossessed: America's Underclasses from the Civil War to the Present (1992), a Choice Academic Book of 1992. Her second book, Labor of Love, Labor of Sorrow: Black Women, Work, and the Family from Slavery to the Present (1985), won the Philip Taft Award in Labor History and the Bancroft Prize in American History, along with several other awards. Professor Jones is currently completing American Work: A Social History.

A friend once suggested to me that all historical scholarship is a form of autobiography—it's just that some autobiographies are better disguised than others. So how did I, the product of a white, middle-class household in a Middle Atlantic state, come to write about black and white sharecroppers, turpentine workers and Appalachian migrants, domestic servants and auto workers? I will let you be the judge about what, if anything, autobiography has to do with it.

Of course we must begin with a particular time and place. In the 1950s Christiana, Delaware, amounted to little more than a rural crossroads, its one intersection the site of a tiny general store, a liquor store, and a fire station. Within a block or two were four small churches and a public elementary school. Christiana had its own post office, but it was never incorporated as a town; with the exception of a school board, it had no public officials and offered no town services. When I looked up the town in an atlas once I was surprised to see its population listed as 500; my family knew virtually everyone in Christiana, and it was hard for us to account for that many people. I suspect about half that number lived there.

Located between Wilmington and Newark, Christiana lay at the northern tip of the coastal plain known as the Delmarva Peninsula; it more closely resembled a rural "downstate" town than one of the suburbs north of Wilmington, home to DuPont Company executives and chemists. The town, with the Christina River snaking through it, had reached its zenith some two hundred years before, when it served as a lively port for goods shipped downstream to Wilmington. Apparently the Marquis de Lafayette deployed his troops on the site during the Revolution, and legend had it that George Washington once slept in a big red brick colonial house not far from ours. When I was growing up, all of this activity in the town was hard to imagine. By this time the river was little more than a muddy stream—a

*Autobiography and Scholarship*

creek, a sorry trickle of a thing—and the town had a distinctly backwater feel to it.

We lived in Christiana because that was where my grandparents had settled in the early 1920s. My grandfather, a land surveyor, spent the first two decades of the twentieth century working for railroad companies in the coal mining regions of the Appalachian Mountains (my mother and her seven siblings were born in five different states, Massachusetts, Pennsylvania, Virginia, West Virginia, and Kentucky). In the course of his travels he discovered a gravel and sand pit in Christiana; he decided to buy it, along with a large parcel of land, and settle his family there. In the 1930s he built what was by local standards a large white frame house near his business. When my mother married in 1945, he gave her and my father a piece of land next to his house.

The gravel pit was full of water, and by the time I was born trees had grown up on all sides; it was no longer dredged for stones and sand to be used in the construction of Wilmington office buildings. We called it the pond, and it served as the emotional and social site of my childhood. My two brothers and my cousins, friends, and I spent endless summer days swimming and fishing there; in the winter we would build a bonfire on the frozen shore and ice-skate by moonlight. The woods behind the pond went on endlessly, perfect places to build forts and concoct fantastic games about Indian scouts and warriors. I used to think that this tiny piece of water—no more than an acre or so in size—was the most beautiful place on earth; it was both a playground and a sanctuary.

The school I attended had one class for each of its six grades; it was a poor school, with no kindergarten, or music, or art—any kind of what we today call "enrichment" classes—for the first four or five years I attended. On my way home every day I would stop at the general store for an orange soda, then walk another quarter of a mile or so to my grandmother's house and visit with her and one of my aunts who came to see her every afternoon. I often spent Saturday mornings poking around my grandfather's office (still filled with his surveying tools; he had died in 1953), reading copies of the *Saturday Evening Post* and exploring the deserted chicken coop and huge garage used to store gravel trucks behind the house.

Both of my maternal grandparents had been born in Massachusetts; my grandfather was descended from William Phelps, who arrived with John Winthrop in the Massachusetts Bay Colony in 1630 and seven years after that led a party of settlers to Connecticut, where he was one of the founders of the town of Windsor. My husband would later wonder how a family that arrived in this country so early could squander its relative advantages. It is true that when I was older and aware of an upper-middle class world, I came to think of Christiana, and my whole existence there, as old-fashioned and a bit shabby in comparison. But at the time my extended family's chief claim to status was our New England roots and my grandparents' prominent place in the local Presbyterian Church. Raised as Congregationalists in Northampton and Worcester, they had to settle for a Presbyterian minister when they moved to Christiana. The small, graceful white stucco building, with its austere interior, had been built in the nineteenth century; the church itself had been founded during the First Great Awakening of the 1740s. My grandparents, my parents, and three of my aunts and their families were pillars of that church. At times it seemed that the Phelpses *were* the church.

The lessons I learned there were at once comforting and terrifying. The minister preached an unadulterated form of Calvinism (George Whitefield would have approved), and I lay in bed more than one night pondering the implications of sanctification and predestination and the possibility that I would burn in hell for eternity. This was stern stuff for a ten-year-old. At times the minister would veer away from biblical doctrine in his sermon and denounce the arrogance of the federal government and the sinfulness of all who called upon it to solve their own problems (especially after 1960); that message fit in well with my extended family's rock-ribbed Republicanism. My grandfather was an even-tempered person, but he had made no secret of the fact that he despised Franklin Roosevelt and all he stood for. My sweet grandmother, a Smith College graduate, liked to watch the Phillies on television and work on complicated word puzzles after she had finished her housework each day; but she still smarted at the insult that Eleanor Roosevelt— that "busybody of a first lady"—had inflicted on her and on all American taxpayers. More generally, I got the impression that when it came to party politics, policy counted for less than "culture"; Republicans stood for upright individualism and accountability and for a sort of self-righteous respectability, while the Democrats were, oddly enough, actually proud of not being able to take care of themselves. At least that was the message I heard when my relatives talked about politics.

Sunday afternoons were the high point of my week. It was then that all of my cousins on my mother's side would descend on my grandmother's house, the children to play together, the aunts and uncles and my grandmother to gossip and discuss the sermon they had heard that morning. In the summer we would play croquet on the lawn and then go swimming or find some frogs to torment. In the fall we would build teepees out of cornstalks in my father's big vegetable garden; and in the spring we would venture across the road and go exploring in the unfamiliar woods. These weekly gatherings represented all that was familiar and dear to me.

Later, a friend of mine (he had grown up in Co-op City and then moved to Queens) would rather scornfully suggest that I had grown up in a Norman Rockwell painting. In the early 1970s I considered this a very serious charge indeed and realized that it would be difficult to defend myself against it: How could I, when I grew up in a house located on East Main Street? Was my childhood really just some awful Rockwellian nightmare of bland security and soul-suffocating conformity? It is true that even Catholics were exotic creatures in Christiana; and, predictably, I never met anyone who was Jewish until I was well along in high school. (I later compensated for this misfortune by marrying a Jewish man and converting to Judaism; so much for Presbyterian indoctrination.)

In any case, I begin with this view of Christiana because it serves to remind me that a picture of a time and place can be accurate, and yet fundamentally false at the same time. Everything I have said about the town thus far is true to the best of my recollection; the quaint village is one that outsiders might have seen, and it is the one that a historian might describe. Yet it does not reveal the essence of the town at all, for the essence of Christiana was its secrets. I call them secrets because they constituted the web of social relations based on assumptions that were referred to only obliquely, if at all, in the course of everyday life. Lodged in these secrets were the passions and prejudices that made Christiana ultimately a more intriguing, if far less pleasant, place than the Rockwellian version would suggest. I think that the only people who romanticize small-town life are the people who have never lived in one; when historians extol the alleged virtues of tight-knit little "communities," I remain skeptical.

Christiana was an arena of social conflict and cultural tensions, a place filled with sexual danger and raw racial prejudice. In trying to sort out these crosscurrents of town life, I am struck by the difficulty of labeling one kind of relationship "racial" and another "class," of separating sexual issues from religious issues, of deciding where one's kin loyalties left off and one's "cultural" sensibilities began, of pulling politics away from economics. But in the interests of (social) science, I'll try.

I now realize that as a child I saw the world organized around the two poles identified by Robert and Helen Lynd

*Autobiography and Scholarship*

in *Middletown*, their classic study of Muncie, Indiana, in the mid-1920s. The Lynds found that the great divide in Muncie was the distinction between the business class and the working class. Although this typology is simplistic, it has a certain appeal, because it allows us to begin with the concrete way people organize their lives every day. And that was my perspective as a youngster growing up in Christiana.

My father and grandfather were two of few professionals in the town. Most of the other men were employed as laborers, or as assembly line workers at one of the local auto plants in Newark or Wilmington. My friends' fathers were routinely afflicted with what they rather mysteriously referred to as "layoffs"; to me that meant that they stayed home—sometimes for weeks at a time—every once in a while. My father, a lower-level manager employed by DuPont, earned a salary; he did not make much money, but he was never laid off. I could sense the tension in the households of my friends when their fathers were out of work; I dreaded seeing them there when we came home from school, sitting off in the corner of the living room, or at the kitchen table, a sullen presence we tried to ignore as "American Bandstand" blared from the TV. My father wore a suit and tie to work; he went off to the office at eight and came home at five; he sat at a desk and talked on the phone, went to meetings, and used an adding machine all day. My friends' fathers wore overalls to work, they usually left early in the morning and arrived home at three or four; but sometimes they had to work the nightshift, and then we had to keep the daytime TV down low so they could sleep in the afternoon.

There were no June Cleavers in the Christiana I knew. My mother, an English major in college, had aspired to be a writer, but when her three children were growing up she worked from time to time as a substitute teacher and wrote articles for two papers, one in Wilmington and one in Newark. She used to tell me that knowing how to write a good

Jacqueline Jones

sentence was the most important skill one could have in life; that was the guiding principle of her life, and our house was perpetually messy, cluttered with books and papers. I inherited from her a lamentably low opinion of housework of all kinds. To me the main contrast between my mother's life and the life of my friends' mothers was that in the 1950s we were able to buy a clothes dryer; my friends' backyards were always festooned with drying clothes flapping in the wind. I somehow connected our abundance of appliances— electric blankets, a hi-fi system, a dishwashing machine, a mangle ironing machine, even an electric knife—with the fact that my father was never laid off.

Within the Christiana working class were several subgroups. One was the Methodists, members of the other white church in town. At the time, I identified the Methodists exclusively with the working-class group, though this was probably a misperception on my part. My Presbyterian kinfolk considered the Methodists too emotional, too little tortured by the doctrine of original sin, and representative of things Southern in a place where we as transplanted New Englanders always felt slightly out of place. In fact, Christiana was home to a number of migrants from West Virginia, Kentucky, and Tennessee, families that had moved north in search of jobs in the auto assembly plants—Chrysler in Newark, General Motors near Wilmington, and assorted box and paper factories scattered throughout the area. The migrants were readily identifiable by their Southern accents, by the chickens and goats they kept in their backyards, and by their regular patronage of the county farmers' market, an indoor flea market that took place in New Castle, a few miles away, each Friday and Saturday night.

I had a number of friends who hailed from the areas around Memphis and Nashville. It was in their homes that I first heard Kitty Wells and Hank Williams on the radio; my parents kept the dial tuned to Bing Crosby, Frank Sinatra, and my mother's all-time favorite, Perry Como. They ate fried chicken and homemade cakes; at our house we had

*Autobiography and Scholarship*

hamburgers and hot dogs and store-bought cookies. From my southern friends I learned how to jitterbug to the tune of "Mama's little baby loves shortnen' bread," and I heard the latest gossip about Elvis Presley, much of it salacious and at least some of it untrue. This was my window onto a world that my relatives clearly disapproved of.

Like all small towns Christiana had a secret sex life. My sharp ears picked up whisperings of unlucky high school girls who had to be packed off to Baltimore to deliver their unwanted babies, my sharp eyes spied the graffiti on the brick walls of the school, with bad words associated with people I knew. A friend who told me about the "games" she played with her uncle I realize now was telling me about her own sexual abuse at his hands. One day, in response to my insistent questions, my father had to admit that the school janitor was fired because he had done some bad things to girls in the custodian's closet. The mother of one of my friends abruptly left the family, her youngest of four children in tow, early one morning. Her husband had a bad temper, and I had more than once seen it in action; I made all sorts of connections. And Christiana had its own little coterie of what we called "hoods," the tough kids who left the church parking lot strewn with beer bottles every Saturday night, who hung out with my friends' older sisters, girls in tight sweaters who, like the boys, mastered the fine art of talking with a cigarette hanging out of their mouth.

Yet even more than the business class–working class divide, a chasm between blacks and whites split the town into clearly identifiable, visibly estranged, groups. The black people who lived in Christiana were segregated on a back road called Brown's Lane; they had their own churches—a black Baptist church, and one of the African Methodist Episcopal Zion denomination. Though they lived within a block or so of the school I attended, until 1956 the black kids had to travel to another town, Newport, where they went to the Absalom Jones school; Delaware had written the racial seg-

Jacqueline Jones

regation of its schools into the state constitution. At the general store and on sidewalks, southern patterns of "racial etiquette" prevailed; black people of all ages and both sexes were supposed to defer to whites and remain as unobtrusive as possible.

The houses on Brown's Lane were very modest, and I suspect that most of the men and women who lived there worked as day laborers or as service employees. They constituted yet another subset of the town's working class, but there was a crucial difference between this group and other wage workers, the Methodists, and the migrants; patterns of racial segregation testified to a general social segregation, and white and black people no matter what their age did not visit each other in their homes.

The civil rights revolution swept through the Delaware school system relatively early—the state was one of the original defendants in the Brown v. Board of Education Supreme Court case in 1954—and when I was in third grade (in 1955) a few black pupils began to attend my school. One day, after the pupils in my class had been paired up to work on a special project, one of the white boys came to school and announced to the teacher that his mother had forbidden him to work with a black partner. This statement prompted a brief discussion in the classroom, with the teacher (one whom I adored) acknowledging that, in Christiana, interracial friendships were not now possible but that "maybe they will be acceptable sometime in the future."

I think her words had a great impact on me, for they alluded both to a mysterious past—one that had brought us to this impasse—and to an uncertain future—one that could presumably turn out quite differently from the present. Perhaps if I could figure out what had happened in the past, things could be different in the future. It was a naive, childish idea, but probably a formative one for me, and I never really outgrew it.

Gradually, I became an avid collector of the town's many secrets, and I became impressed with the sheer melodramatic quality of it all; under a cover of church-going piety and serenity lay an ugly pile of hypocrisy mixed with, as far as I could tell, a fair dose of godlessness. This discovery filled me with a feeling of self-righteousness, and after that no act of generosity could redeem the town in my eyes, a point brought home every Thanksgiving Day. Ever since I could remember the black and white churches got together that holiday morning for a joint service, rotated year to year among the four of them, with the host preacher in charge. It was a wonderful experience for me to go to that service and sit on wooden pews in one of the three churches that I walked past nearly every day but entered only once every four years. Nevertheless, any sense of wonder I derived from the experience would quickly dissipate later in the day when, after the traditional turkey dinner, we would all gather at my grandmother's house for dessert. There my relatives would ridicule the fellow congregants they had encountered in the morning; the Methodists sang too loud, and their preacher went in for theatrics; the black worshippers actually called out "Amen!" in the course of the sermon, and even worse, swayed a little when they sang. An hour of superficial racial harmony yielded an afternoon of collective, extended-family sanctimony; as a family we reaffirmed who we were by setting ourselves apart from everybody else.

And so where outsiders (like my friend from Co-op City) might have seen only the dull sweetness of small-town life, I saw a cauldron of seething conflicts, as people put other people into categories and organized their view of the world accordingly; perhaps the real divide in the town separated people who resisted such categorization from those who insisted on perpetuating it. In any case, I became a social historian.

Over the past twenty years, I have written three books in the field of African American history, and each one grew out of an initial misapprehension, a faulty premise, about the American political economy, past and present. I have no regrets about writing any of those books, but at times I felt I was learning more from them than I wanted to; they were an exercise in disillusionment.

In terms of politics, I remained a dutiful daughter through high school. My senior social studies teacher, a notorious liberal, once assigned me the task of writing a research report on the so-called culture of poverty. Michael Harrington's *The Other America* had been published a few years earlier (1962), and I read it and then wrote approvingly of the idea that most poor folks did not really want to improve their own lives; they reveled in their own misery. A year later I found myself entering the University of Delaware—not exactly a hotspot in the landscape of radicalism in the 1960s, but the site of my conversion from Eisenhower Republicanism to something that had no partisan political label, since Lyndon Johnson had forever tainted the Democrats with his prosecution of the Vietnam War. I had left Christiana for good. Although the town was only five miles away, I went home to visit only every once in a while.

During my last two years at college, my intellectual interests began to coalesce around African American history. I coordinated a student project that combined a course in urban sociology with university student-run tutorials for black kids in Wilmington every Saturday afternoon; this project was an obvious attempt to link scholarship with social activism, no matter how innocuous its form. In the classroom, I was restless and bored with my major in American Studies until I was fortunate enough to take the very first course in black history taught at Delaware. The professor was Thomas Cripps, who had to be imported each week from Morgan State, a black college in Baltimore. Cripps was tremendously knowledgeable about black history, and he introduced me to a way of looking at the past that I found intellectually exciting, in contrast to the emphasis on traditional political history that pervaded all of my other classes. After taking his course, and in conjunction with the inner-city tutoring project, I was inspired to write a senior essay on a subject I stumbled across in the library one day—the history of the Delaware Association for the Moral Improvement and Education of the Colored People, a philanthropic organization founded by Wilmington Quakers around the time of the Civil War; they raised money for black schools in the state because black children were barred by law from attending tax-supported schools of any kind. I located the minutes of the group in the Delaware Historical Society, and the report I wrote became my first publication—in a 1972 issue of *Delaware History*.

My interest in the history of African American education led directly to the topic of my dissertation and of my first book, a study of the northern teachers who went south after the Civil War to teach the freedpeople of Georgia. These women were the daughters of New England Protestant farmers, tradesmen, and clergymen; most had some formal teacher training or teaching experience; and all of them were imbued with the desire to become "useful" during this time of military and political upheaval. For obvious reasons I found the teachers' stories appealing and even vaguely familiar. I too believed firmly in the regenerative power of formal education and in the moral transcendence of personal encounters between blacks and whites.

However, the more I learned about the teachers' experiences in Georgia, the more I realized I was wrong, that my whole study was based on a misplaced faith in schools and in the goodwill of white people. African Americans in Georgia (and throughout the South) embraced literacy as an essential component of freedom; but without land, capital, or credit, they remained vulnerable to the depredations of whites of all social classes. The teachers might preach the virtues of thrift and hard work to their pupils, young, and old, but the white women were sadly mistaken in their conviction that personal virtue would inevitably yield to land-ownership and political power. And the teachers' "maternalism"—their well-meaning but condescending treatment

Jacqueline Jones

of black people—struck me as but another variation on the themes of racial and class prejudice. I had intended to write a book that might illuminate our own time; and instead I ended up with a cautionary tale, convinced of the utter futility of the teachers' best intentions within the context of the postbellum South, and skeptical of any missionary's message that preached racial equality but omitted mention of economic inequality.

In the process of researching *Soldiers of Light and Love*, I found myself more interested in the everyday struggles of the Georgia freedpeople than in the work of the teachers in the classroom. And in 1976, faced with a paucity of published materials to assign students in my women's history class at Wellesley College, I decided to write a survey of black women's work and family life. In the process I shifted from my liberal phase to my feminist phase. To me, the story I told in *Labor of Love, Labor of Sorrow* was not only a powerful story in its own right—the determination of African American women to resist the demands that slave owners and employers made upon them, in favor of attending to the needs to their own families—the book also brought together some of the major themes of the "New Social History"—the contributions of women to community life and the significance of the family in shaping patterns of work and culture. The tribulations and triumphs of black women, I believed, stood at the center of American history; in the lives of ordinary black women were conjoined three systems of oppression, based on race, gender, and class.

Alas, I realized even as I was writing the book that my basic assumption was flawed; black women did not stand at the center of the story alone, but together with their kinfolk. In fact, my focus on women seemed inaccurate and ultimately arbitrary. Cutting black men out of the picture, or at least pushing them to the background, produced an account fundamentally at odds with a true rendering of the past. In addition, I was struck by the similarities in the material condition of poor whites and their black counterparts; white

124

sharecroppers had obvious, if only relative, advantages compared to blacks in the late nineteenth-century South, but the day-to-day routines of the households of both groups did not differ that much.

The Dispossessed was an attempt to grapple with class and "race" relations, using the grand sweep of economic transformations over the last century and a half as the backdrop. In illuminating the political dynamics that underlay patterns of black and white poverty, I also wanted to make a contribution to current debates about the nature of the so-called urban black "underclass." It seemed to me that much of the discussion among politicians, policymakers, and social scientists in the 1980s was ahistorical and preoccupied with the notion that black poverty today is somehow unique and "culturally" inevitable. In the course of doing research for the book I had found that many of the same economic forces that afflicted blacks affected poor whites as well, and that the stories of the two groups diverged in some places but converged in many others. Furthermore, as household members, poor people of both races struggled mightily to provide for their own welfare in ways that their social betters could not always comprehend or appreciate.

The book came out in 1992, around the time of the civil disorders in south-central Los Angeles, and I thought it might help to inform a presidential contest that seemed almost based on pushing the plight of poor people off the public agenda. I had ended the book with a discussion of the many distressed communities proliferating throughout the country today in an effort to steer the debate away from the current obsession with "race." My mistake here was the idea that Americans would find this suggestion compelling and that I could somehow insinuate myself into a larger discussion dominated by sociologists and political scientists, people very much taken with the idea of black pathology. I took my cue from Gunnar Myrdal, who in his book American Dilemma suggested that white Americans were ignorant of black history and that a better understanding of that history would pave the way for a more equitable society.

During the summer and fall of 1992 I waited for the calls from Terry Gross, host of "Fresh Air," and Scott Simon of "All Things Considered" on National Public Radio. Certainly my book was worth a review in *The New York Times*, though perhaps hoping for a slot on "Oprah" was too much! In any case, the book failed to capture the imagination (let alone the attention) of the news media or the public (or perhaps I should say the public via the news media). Most people seemed to feel the same way as the prominent "underclass" theorist whom I encountered one day; he told me, "Historians say that we should pay more attention to history, but I don't believe it; we don't seem to be missing a whole lot [by ignoring what happened in the past]."

So much for my attempt to connect with the American electorate. Many of my tradition-minded colleagues would say that the impulse was inappropriate in any case, that trying to make any connection between the past and current social policy inevitably corrupts scholarship. I don't believe that. (Challenging a person's motivation for writing history is a waste of time; focus on his or her footnotes instead.) But I also doubt the wisdom of Myrdal's claim that the historical truth will set us all free. The idea that the American public simply needs a good history lesson strikes me as being as naive and simple-minded as some of the other assumptions that have shaped my career.

Still, hope springs eternal. Today I am completing a book on the social organization of labor throughout American history, focusing on the work of African Americans over the generations and the terms and conditions of their work. It seemed to me that, over the last fifteen or twenty years, labor historians (myself included) had engaged in a process of scholarly self-segregation; books about white workers included a paragraph about blacks and their "uniqueness,"

Autobiography and Scholarship

while most works dealing with blacks pushed whites out of the picture. I wanted to explore the two overlapping systems of labor—black and white—and understand how the shape of one was related to, and influenced, the shape of the other. More generally (and grandly) I wanted to put the history of African American men, women, and children at the moral center of American labor history, beginning with the earliest colonial settlements and coming up to the present.

I have found that, after slavery, in the North beginning around the 1790s and in the South after 1865, whites created an elaborate "racial" mythology that portrayed black people as lazy and at the same time so determined to work that they would not rest until they had stripped white people of their own source of livelihood. This mythology was obviously self-contradictory; it was a ludicrous image, this notion that "shiftless" blacks were also predators, depriving white people of their "rightful" place in society and specifically of their exclusive claim to good schools and good jobs. It was a nineteenth-century variation on what economists call a "zero-sum game"—the idea that the welfare of one group (blacks) necessarily and automatically comes at the expense of another group (whites). We can of course today hear echoes of this ideology in state legislatures and in the presidential primary campaign, and those echoes tell us much about the terms of our "racial discourse"; one side of the coin is the attack on black women as lazy (in a way that supposedly white middle-class women who want to stay home with their children are not), and the other side is the widespread belief among whites that black men (in particular) are "too aggressive" in wanting to find good jobs for themselves and good schools for their children. The two sides are conjoined in current debates over welfare "reform" and affirmative action. (All of the prejudices that shape those debates found succinct expression in a recent best-seller, The Bell Curve.)

But despite the "relevance" of this historical analysis to

Jacqueline Jones

the mess we are in today, I hope I have enough sense not to sit by the phone waiting for Diane Sawyer or Tom Brokaw to call me to talk about it.

Not long ago I was talking about Christiana to a family friend. He started to say something about Christiana as a community and then checked himself to say, "But of course there is no community anymore; there is only the mall."

A half mile out of town now sits a gigantic mall that attracts shoppers from New Jersey, Pennsylvania, Maryland, and all parts of Delaware. The out-of-staters are drawn to Delaware's sales-tax free shopping; the local crowd comes because it is the biggest place around, with four flagship department stores and, as they like to say, "ample free parking." The mall, just off I-95, has long since gobbled up the Lynam family farm, where we used to go to buy our eggs Saturday afternoons. Christiana is now ringed by hundreds of acres of housing developments—apartments, townhouses, and modest single-family homes. There is a little strip shopping center in the middle of town now, but the real action takes place at the mall and at several other large fast-food and discount-store complexes in the immediate vicinity. The house where I grew up is surrounded by great interstate freeway clover-leafs and by congested traffic intersections. The pond is polluted with the run-off from new highways.

Christiana, and all of New Castle County, has changed dramatically over the last two decades because of the expansion in Delaware's financial services industry. People come from up and down the eastern seaboard to find jobs as keypunch operators and tele-marketers for gigantic banks such as MBNA and Chase Manhattan, companies lured to the state by its lax incorporation and tax laws. The quality of new housing built to accommodate the newcomers reveals that the jobs are not very good. Meanwhile, the large

Chrysler and General Motors plants are undergoing extensive upgrading; that means that, as more technology is introduced, more workers will be laid off. DuPont, like all big companies, continues to reduce its workforce and close plant facilities in an effort to streamline. Wilmington, once a vibrant, if small, city, now has the appearance of a post-industrial ghost town. The high-rise office buildings are still there, for the (mostly white) employees of large corporations; but the downtown area has been completely stripped of its commercial core. There are no department stores or restaurants left, only tiny mom-and-pop storefronts operated by black men and women who are trying to eke out an existence with the help of customers of their own race.

Once again, this bleak picture tells only part of the story. Christiana appears, at least, to be much more racially integrated than it used to be. At the mall, black men sport shiny Teamster and UAW jackets; and the crowds at the local roller skating rink, the K-Mart, and the grocery store make it clear that the area has not become just one more lily-white suburb. Yet, for all I know, the churches are just as segregated as they used to be, and black and white kids still don't go over to each other's houses after school. I am certain that the town still has its secrets, some of them new, but many of them simply updated with the times. To me, the town today (whatever is left of it as a community) represents a quintessentially American exurbia of the 1990s—from my own self-absorbed perspective I see it as the epilogue to *The Dispossessed*.

I will continue to write about the issues that intrigue me the most—that is, the issues that connect the American past to the present and to the future. I have always considered the story of African Americans to be the story of America, and I reject the currently fashionable position that declares certain kinds of history off-limits to certain kinds of people. Although I have enjoyed my little stroll down memory lane here today, I hope that most of you will ultimately con-

Jacqueline Jones

sider the town of Christiana irrelevant to the history I write. And to make certain that we relegate the autobiographical aspects of historical scholarship to their proper place, I suggest that we focus not on an author's background but on her footnotes, and avoid reading too much between the lines.

*Autobiography and Scholarship*

# 8. Conclusion: The Significance of the Personal for the Professional

Mark D. Naison is Professor of African American Studies at Fordham University in The Bronx, where he also serves as chair of his department and as the director of the Urban Studies Program. He earned his B.A. in 1966, his M.A. in 1967, and his Ph.D. in 1976 from Columbia University and began teaching at Fordham in 1970. He has held an American Council of Learned Societies fellowship and his book Communists in Harlem during the Depression (1983) won the Ralph J. Bunche Award of the American Political Science Association. He has also edited The Tenant Movement in New York City, 1904–1984 (1986) and was general editor of the microfilm collection "Research Collections in American Radicalism" (1986–1991). Professor Naison has published numerous articles on African American life, including "Outlaw Culture and Black Neighborhoods" (1992) and "Jared Taylor's America: Black Man's Heaven, White Man's Hell" (1994). He continues to research the role of black culture and Communists as well as sport in American life.

The papers in this collection remind us of why African American history has been a source of such intellectual excitement for the last thirty years. The scholars represented here were part of a generation that was inventing a new nation—a multiracial democracy in which people of African descent were full and equal partners. Living through a profound social revolution, they turned to the discipline of history to give the tumultuous changes of their time—in race, in gender, in national identity—a connection to important events in the American past. In so doing, they helped create a language and a set of traditions that could help Americans live more comfortably in their brave new world of political equality and cultural diversity.

As these accounts suggest, the United States was a segregated society well up through the 1950s, a place where discourse on race was marked by stereotypes and assumptions that bore little resemblance to the lived experience of its black population. In the South of George B. Tindall and Dan T. Carter, the intimacy of shared childhoods and common work, spilling over into language, religion, and public recreation, clashed sharply with the official ideology of segregation and white supremacy and the grim adherence to a caste system in politics and education. Were black and white Southerners two distinct peoples, or were they inextricably linked by culture and biology in ways that segregationists sought to deny? For Tindall, the offhand remark of a high school history teacher about the prevalence of African ancestry among the very legislators that introduced segregation drove him to explore the role of African Americans in the paradoxical history of his home state of South Carolina. What he found was a hybrid civilization, a continuum of colors and cultures in which the "white" population was willing to go to extraordinary lengths of violence and po-

132

litical subterfuge to set itself apart. Segregation was not "natural"; an atmosphere of hysteria was required to impose and sustain it, a denial of the powerful historical forces that had linked Europeans and Africans together biologically, culturally, and economically.

For Carter, another white "Carolinian," history became his vehicle for understanding how his friends and neighbors, normally decent and compassionate people, could become cruel and violent when facing challenges to the white supremacist social order they lived in. A civil rights activist in college, Carter chose as subjects moments in which white Southerners rose to defend their caste system against internal and external challenges, writing his first book on the Scottsboro case and his third on the ascent to national prominence of George Wallace. Like Tindall, Carter found that the maintenance of white supremacy in the South required artificially induced levels of political mobilization, a state of constant vigilance lest the normal intimacy of neighbors and coworkers spill over into "social equality." Amidst violence and tragedy, Carter found cultural commonalities among black and white Southerners that made legal integration manageable once the back of Southern resistance was broken by the federal government.

The ironies and cruelties of white supremacist ideology, splendidly revealed by these "Reconstructed" Southerners, had an equal impact on the lives and scholarship of the five Northern contributors to this collection. Leon F. Litwack grew up in a multiracial working-class community whose values and traditions received no recognition in the curriculum of California schools in the 1940s. The child of self-educated working-class radicals, Litwack encountered official history as the triumphal march of Anglo-Saxon civilization, rendering immigrants and people of color invisible and defining African Americans as a people whose one experience with political equality—Reconstruction—justified their marginalized and segregated status. For Litwack, the distortion of the African American experience served as a

Mark D. Naison

metaphor for an elitist and ethnocentric academic culture that excluded all groups that did not leave their imprint on the corridors of power. In his groundbreaking first book, *North of Slavery*, Litwack demonstrated that white supremacist thinking was as deeply entrenched in the "free" North as in the slave-holding South, and that Northern blacks, in the pre–Civil War era, were victims of a vicious system of caste segregation. His account was a chilling reminder of the degree to which the entire American political culture was infused with enthnocentrism, showing how humor, folklore, education and the popular press disseminated images of black inferiority. First published in 1961, *North of Slavery* suggested that the achievement of racial equality required a reformulation of national identity as well as the elimination of discriminatory laws, a task in which historians could play an important role.

David Levering Lewis's upbringing, while more sheltered than Litwack's, displayed the level of racial isolation among even educated and prosperous Northern blacks in the 1940s and 50s. Lewis's family—urbane, cultivated, deeply ambitious for its children—had almost no contact with whites with comparable values. Lewis grew up with the paragons of African American cultural and political life as regular dinner guests and was sent off to Fisk University, where he encountered inspirational teaching and a rigorous curriculum in the arts and sciences. Compulsively curious and profoundly gifted, Lewis, in classic "Talented Tenth" fashion, crafted a career that would shatter the boundaries of his segregated world, pursuing degrees in French history at Columbia and the London School of Economics and spending years as an expatriate scholar in Europe and Africa. Abroad during the civil rights years, Lewis returned to the United States to write a pioneering biography of Martin Luther King, Jr., drawing upon his family's extensive contacts with Atlanta's black elite and the strong parallels between King's upbringing and his own. The success of this book trans-

Conclusion

formed Lewis into a symbol of the newly popular field of African American history, opening up new opportunities for him within American universities. Continuing his scholarship in French history, Lewis undertook another project that dramatized the Talented Tenth's impact on American life, a study of writers of the Harlem Renaissance who saw their artistic achievements as an illustration of their people's aptitude for democratic citizenship. By the time his groundbreaking biography of W. E. B. Du Bois had been published in 1993, Lewis had helped carve a place for the African American intelligentsia in the mainstream of cultural history, sensitizing scholars to the accomplishments of an embattled, often isolated group of blacks that kept alive the ideals of liberal education in a segregated world.

Eric Foner, though superficially a white suburbanite, grew up in a family milieu that was as insulated from traditional American perspectives on race as was David Levering Lewis's. Foner's parents, Communist Party activists, had adopted racial equality as a political and moral imperative twenty years before the Montgomery bus boycott and had been blacklisted from the teaching profession for their political beliefs. For Foner, becoming a civil rights activist in the sixties was a natural extension of his "family values"; demonstrations against racial discrimination and lectures on African American history had been more a part of his upbringing than Elvis Presley and Marilyn Monroe. At Columbia University, Foner became a leader of the campus civil rights movement, but he also became interested in writing American history. Unlike many of his peers, Foner viewed American perspectives on race with the curiosity of an outsider rather than the passions of the true believer; and he was capable of meticulously and dispassionately analyzing popular movements that combined democratic rhetoric and anti-black sentiments.

Foner's first book, *Free Soil, Free Labor, Free Men*, showed how the protection of free white labor served as the rallying cry

Mark D. Naison

for the movement to contain the expansion of slavery and how most Free Soil leaders excluded African Americans from their vision of an ideal American republic. For many Northern whites, Foner shrewdly observed, a society without slavery meant a society without blacks. Two of Foner's subsequent books, *Tom Paine and Revolutionary America* and *Reconstruction*, also explored the limits of democratic ideology in American society. His study of Reconstruction, the definitive work on the subject, highlighted the difficulties of securing political freedom for a newly emancipated people without a firm economic foundation for their liberty. Foner's ability to maintain ironic distance from national myths without sentimentalizing the nation's victims has made him one of the most respected historians of our time. Through all his awards and honors, he has held to the central insight of his "un-American" parents—that the experience of African Americans has shaped everything Americans have done—from conquering a new land, to writing a constitution, to building an industrial economy.

Jacqueline Jones's upbringing, radically different from Foner's, dramatizes the role of the civil rights movement in transforming the lives of young people brought up in Cold War America. Jones, the author of several brilliant works on African American and women's history, came to the same conclusions as Foner about the centrality of race in the shaping of American identity despite a conservative, small-town background and family roots that go back to the Puritans. Amidst church suppers, sock-hops, and dips in the local swimming hole, Jones noticed that her Delaware town was minutely divided by race and class and that its sense of community was undermined by jealousy and fear. Mandatory school integration brought these tensions to the surface, convincing Jones that moral rectitude and individual self-improvement—the values preached by her middle-class, Republican relatives—did little to explain the lives of her African American and working-class white neighbors. In

Conclusion

college, Jones became involved in community service work in a black community and took her first course in African American history. These experiences helped convince her to write history that projected outsiders and neglected groups—women, African Americans, working-class people—into the center of America's historical development.

Jones's first book, *Soldiers of Light and Love*, looked at the experience of northern female teachers who went down to work with Georgia's freedpeople after the Civil War; her second book, *Labor of Love, Labor of Sorrow*, explored the lives of African American women from slavery to the present; her third book, *The Dispossessed*, examined the lives of economically marginalized families of all races who had difficulty achieving the American dream. In these works, Jones shattered the image of small-town, agrarian America as a crucible of egalitarian values; she revealed a community consensus shaped as much by race and class prejudice as democratic opportunity. Those who invoke a Golden Age of American harmony as a bulwark against the tumultuous present have found a formidable opponent in Jacqueline Jones.

Darlene Clark Hine's contribution to this collection, unlike those of the other six scholars, is the product of a post–civil rights experience. Hine's formative intellectual experiences took shape within the Black Power movement, a milieu that self-consciously rejected the aesthetic and political conditions for racial integration that civil rights leaders had espoused. Inspired by the imperative to create academic and cultural organizations guided by African American values and traditions, she turned to the study of history to uncover patterns of life and thought through which African Americans shaped their adaptation to a hostile society.

In working on her first book, a study of the white primary in Texas, Hine acquired new respect for people she had once disdained as racial moderates, civil rights activists who painstakingly chipped away at the logic of a segregated

Mark D. Naison

society. While the black revolutionaries of her generation fell prey to government repression and internecine violence, Hine found solace in the accomplishments of NAACP lawyers of the 1930s and 1940s, concluding that "the most transformative . . . social deeds are often the actions of . . . individuals who possess oppositional consciousness and a mastery of the skills essential to their chosen profession." For Hine, the decline of revolutionary possibilities spawned an appreciation of the role historical writing might play in the shaping of a new society.

Hine continued her historical research on black professionals and then was drawn into a project examining the history of black women in Indiana. Bringing a group into the mainstream of historical study, she soon discovered, was very much like incorporating them into a political community from which they had been excluded. African American history, itself a new field, contained a powerful gender bias—archives, oral histories, even definitions of political resistance all highlighted the experience of African American men. To recapture a tradition of culture-building and resistance among black women, Hine had to collect source materials scattered throughout private homes and decode activities which had previously been ignored as objects of historical study—childrearing practices, domestic rituals, forms of shared labor and childcare, and minutes of associations representing heavily female professions. The book she wrote on culture and community among black women in Indiana helped create an entirely new field of historical study—black women's history—which has become an important focus of teaching and research at American universities. Hine advanced this field not only through the force of her own scholarship (she wrote a subsequent book on black women in the nursing profession) but by developing outlets for other scholars doing research on black women— editing an anthology, sponsoring conferences, developing archives, and producing an encyclopedia. Her work puts her

Conclusion

squarely in the tradition of Carter G. Woodson, W. E. B. Du Bois, John Hope Franklin, and August Meier, pioneers who created a legacy of scholarship in African American history of such unassailable professionalism and intellectual breadth that no synthesis of American history—from a high school textbook to a presidential address to the Organization of American Historians—can afford to exclude it.

In reviewing the work of these seven scholars, one is struck by the power of historical scholarship to give substance and permanence to processes of contemporary social change. When historically disadvantaged groups demand full inclusion in a society, as African Americans did in the 1950s and 60s, their actions are often profoundly destabilizing on an individual and collective level. Because symbols of the groups' "inferiority" have been deeply embedded in folklore and popular culture, the achievement of political equality does not easily translate into social or cultural equality. The civil rights revolution symbolized by the passage of the Voting Rights Act of 1965 did not usher in a new era of racial harmony in the United States; rather, it initiated a protracted, often violent conflict over the status of blacks within the educational system, the media, the labor market, and the culture of families and neighborhoods. The bitter, frightening nature of these conflicts left many activists disillusioned and many citizens confused. Why were race relations so bad after an unprecedented era of social reform? Why did the legacy of past injustices continue to haunt us at a time when legal inequality had finally been uprooted from American life?

For the last thirty years, historians have addressed these questions through the discipline of scholarship, creating a detailed and nuanced portrait of the power of race in shaping the American past. Their work constitutes an attempt to build living traditions of discourse on race rooted in a striving for objectivity, a tradition of civility among discussants, and a dialogue between present and past that focuses on

Mark D. Naison

sources and facts rather than the racial identity of the participants. In the post–civil rights years, black and white historians have published hundreds of books and thousands of articles examining the African American presence in American politics and culture. Our multiracial society now has a multiracial history as a reference point for its conflicts and strivings, and a group of historians who have learned to transcend racial barriers in pursuit of knowledge.

For me, joining this community of scholars represented an act of faith that Martin Luther King, Jr.'s dream of an interracial society could somehow be rescued from the rage and resentment that came to dominate race relations in the mid-1960s. As a child growing up in the Brooklyn of the 1950s, racial issues did not deeply impress themselves on my consciousness. My family, lower-middle-class Jewish liberals, did not use racial epithets in daily conversation, and my neighborhood peer group of arrow-shooting, stickball playing, sports-mad friends included two African Americans (out of about twenty). Equally important, my cultural heroes—athletes and rock and roll stars—were totally interracial, and my friends and I never mentioned race when extolling the virtues of our favorites (Willie Mays vs Mickey Mantle; Little Anthony and the Imperials vs Dion and the Belmonts!). However, this "color-blind" period of my life came to an abrupt end when I entered high school and confronted a large group of black students bussed into my largely Jewish and Italian neighborhood from Bedford Stuyvesant. Many white kids in the school resented the large black presence and showed their displeasure either through acts of violence or—more common among my friends—by keeping as far away from the black students as they could. In turn, some black kids found it extremely tempting to harass middle-class white kids who were smaller, younger, and obviously afraid of them. In gym class, I became the target of some teasing by six older black kids and got knocked unconscious in the fight that followed. When my parents found out about this, they forced me to transfer into an elite

Conclusion

academic high school in an adjoining neighborhood which was still overwhelmingly white.

Although this incident abruptly ended my "age of innocence," it triggered more curiosity than hostility. There was a civil rights group at my new high school, composed largely of children of Communists, that was working with black ministers in Brooklyn to challenge discrimination in housing and employment. I started attending some meetings and made plans to attend a demonstration at a Brooklyn bakery notorious for its lily-white hiring practices. When I told my parents about my plans, they responded with an outpouring of rage about "the shwvartzes taking over Brooklyn" and "ruining everything they touched." "If you want to help someone, do something for the Jews," they proclaimed. Their response, shocking in its intensity, made me more determined to attend the demonstration and more willing to see the struggle for racial justice, now a daily presence on the evening news, as something relevant to the North as well as the South.

In college, my evolution as a civil rights activist was temporarily postponed by the demands of competitive tennis and the joys of an active social life. But after reading James Baldwin's *Another Country* and listening to Martin Luther King's speech at the March on Washington, I joined Columbia CORE in the beginning of my sophomore year and marched down to East Harlem to work as a tutor and a tenant organizer. The richness and variety of CORE's activities—rent strikes, "sandwich tests" to expose housing discrimination, sit-ins and stall-ins to desegregate schools, unionization drives among low-wage workers—convinced me that the civil rights movement was the center of a process of political renewal in the United States. In my classes in American history, which included no books on African American history, I sought out research projects with a civil rights component. As a junior, I did a paper on the "Disfranchisement of the Negro in Alabama" which used, as a source, the three-foot-high Proceedings of the Alabama

*Mark D. Naison*

Constitutional Convention of 1901 whose pages crumbled in my fingers every time I touched them. The excitement of reliving this history, using a source that no one at Columbia had thought to look at, sent chills through me. The life of a historian suddenly assumed great moral appeal—writing history and making history could be effortlessly woven together in a life dedicated to the struggle for racial justice.

However, events in my personal life soon imparted a more somber cast to my political vision. In the second half of my senior year, I fell in love with a black woman I was dating. When I told my parents of my feelings, they became hysterical; my mother threatened suicide and my father told me there was no place in the family if this young woman was with me. Hurt and enraged, I broke all economic ties with them, living off summer jobs and the fellowship I received for graduate work and establishing common residence with my friend in an apartment near Columbia.

Being part of an interracial couple in the late 60s was an exercise in guerrilla theater. My girlfriend's family, half located in Georgia, half located in New York, accepted us enthusiastically—we had wonderful family outings and always had a place at Christmas and Thanksgiving. Teenagers we worked with in community programs—whether black, white, or Hispanic—loved us, sometimes moving in with us temporarily when family pressures got too great. But some black college students, caught up in the passions of the Black Power movement, made our lives extremely difficult; even individuals friendly to me made my girlfriend feel like a "race traitor" for having a white boyfriend. The accumulated pressures of disapproval from black peers, ostracism from my family, and the remarkable array of looks and comments we received when walking down the street made me feel that race was at the heart of a profound national pathology. The prospect of black people and white people living together, socializing together, and marrying one another had the power to turn otherwise decent people into raving lunatics. This was really interesting! This was some-

Conclusion

thing that could take a lifetime of historical research to understand!

Determined to find alternatives to the politics of rage and polarization, I began choosing research subjects that explored moments of interracial solidarity in American history. For my master's thesis, I did a study of the Southern Tenant Farmers' Union, an interracial movement of agricultural workers in the Mississippi Delta during the Depression years. For my dissertation, I explored the racial policies of the American Communist Party, the first political movement in American history to encourage intermarriage between blacks and whites and define fraternization between the races as central to the emancipation of the poor. In undertaking these projects, I could place myself in the context of a long line of individuals who had challenged racial taboos and paid a price for their beliefs but who had expanded the boundaries of freedom in an ethnocentric society. When conducting interviews for my project, I met people who had been fighters for racial justice for sixty years, who had survived whippings, jailings, cross-burnings, loss of employment, FBI harassment, and desertion by friends and relatives and still looked back on their life with joy and gratitude.

My book, Communists in Harlem during the Depression, published by the University of Illinois Press in 1983, documented the prominent role of such radicals in establishing a tradition of interracial solidarity in the nation's largest urban center. The Communist Party, a small, largely immigrant organization, captured the imagination of the Harlem community in the 1930s by mobilizing its largely white constituency to march side by side with blacks in hunger marches, to picket establishments that discriminated against black patrons, and to attend large "interracial dances" that dramatized the Party's contempt for American racial taboos. Ironically, Soviet influence had much to do with the Party's vanguard stance. It required successive "Resolutions on the Negro Question" jointly drafted by black Communists and

143

Mark D. Naison

Soviet nationality experts to make interracial solidarity and support for racial equality a moral imperative in communist circles. But when Harlemites saw thousands of white Communists marching through their neighborhood demanding freedom for the Scottsboro boys; when they saw interracial teams of Communists moving back the furniture of evicted families; when they saw public trials of white Communists accused of insulting their African American comrades, they began to feel less isolated and embattled, to see cracks in an edifice of white supremacy that had previously seemed impregnable.

The Party's pioneering initiatives on race, Harlemites soon discovered, coexisted with practices ranging from the unfamiliar to the offensive. The Party's adulation of everything Soviet, its propensity to view all forms of opposition as treason, and the rigid, hierarchical character of its meetings and public ceremonies (in contrast to the freewheeling, often contentious atmosphere in African American organizations) led many African Americans to keep Communists at arm's length. But by showing Harlemites that interracial solidarity was possible, Communists helped make black community leaders—particularly ministers, politicians, and heads of fraternal organizations—more receptive to alliances with organized labor and more willing to use militant protest tactics. By the end of the Depression, Harlem was a community in upheaval, in protest against police brutality, against white control of its commercial district, and against discrimination practiced by schools, hospitals, and public utilities. In addition, Communists helped prod liberal whites, within the intelligentsia and mainstream religious denominations, to be far more aggressive in challenging racial discrimination. By the time the United States entered World War II, racial barriers were beginning to fall in the arts, in organized sports, and the trade union movement, while important Northern political leaders such as Fiorello La Guardia were beginning to espouse the goal of an integrated society. Failures as revolutionaries, Communists helped reinvigorate traditions of interracial popular protest that had been dormant since Populism, thus helping to set the stage for the civil rights offensive of the postwar years.

It took ten difficult years to write *Communists in Harlem* as a dissertation and as a book. While writing it, I was lucky enough to have mentors who respected my political passions but insisted that my historical writing meet the highest standards of rigor and objectivity. Under the guidance of Nathan Huggins, Eric Foner, James Shenton, and August Meier (my editor at University of Illinois Press), I learned to track down every possible source, make corrections for my own biases, avoid extraneous political commentary, display empathy for those I was writing about, and above all, to place my work in the context of scholars who came before me. Only by respecting the norms of the profession, they argued, could my work have lasting value, could it contribute to the way historians, and ultimately the American public, viewed the impact of race on American identity. Although I sometimes chafed under their strictures, I came to draw comfort from prodecures assuring distance and objectivity, to see the slow pace of historical scholarship as a healing element in a discourse on race too often marked by hyperbole and hysteria.

Today, the body of work by authors represented in this collection is one of the most valuable legacies of the civil rights era. Although the media continue to annoint demagogues and extremists as spokespersons on black history (all of my students have heard of Leonard Jeffries, few of John Hope Franklin), our universities contain hundreds of scholars whose writings on African American history embody deep moral commitments, an appreciation of irony and ambiguity, rigorous documentation, and respect for evidence. The work they have produced has left the current generation of students with an accurate and varied picture

Mark D. Naison

of the African presence in America from the first years of conquest and settlement through the troubled and tumultuous present. This is a legacy to be cherished, the intellectual foundation of a multiracial political community based on tolerance and mutual respect.

Conclusion

# Index

program of, 55, 64–65n.1; Hine
on murders of leaders of, 55–56
Black Power movement: and develop-
ment of black history, 55, 137
*Black Reconstruction* (Du Bois, 1935), 19
Blacks: legal definition of race in
South, 8; exclusion of from
American history and identity,
16; Black Consciousness Move-
ment and identity of, 53. *See also*
Black history; Race; Racism
*Black Victory: The Rise and Fall of the
White Primary in Texas* (Hine,
1979), 56–59
*Black Women in America: An Historical
Encyclopedia* (Hine, 1993), 59,
63–64
Black Women in the Middle West
project, 60
*Black Women in White: Racial Conflict and
Cooperation in the Nursing Profession,
1890 to 1950* (Hine, 1989), 59–63
Blassingame, John, 67
Blues: and black experience in the
South, 26–28
Boritt, Gabor, 92–93
Branch, Taylor, 68
Brown, Sterling, 26
Brown, Willie, 27
*Brown v. Board of Education* (1954), 120
Bruce, Dickson, 68
Buchanan, Scott, 72
Burgess, John W., 104
Bush, George, 47

Caldwell, Erskine, 36
Campbell, Rev. Will, 42
Carlyle, Thomas, 71
Carter, Dan T.: biography of, 33–34;
on race relations and white South-
ern culture, 34–50; personal expe-
rience and approach to race and
history, 132, 133
Carter, Jimmy, 46
Carver, George Washington, 93
Catholic Church: Lewis on modern-
ization in twentieth-century
France and, 77–78
Chicago Historical Society, 106–107

City College: intellectual community of, in 1970s, 100
Civil rights movement: impact of,
on attitudes toward segregation in
the South, 12; and class issues,
13; impact of, on study of American history, 22–23; Litwack on
gains and failures of, 28–29; Carter on role of Arthur and Muriel
Lewis in Alabama, 48–50; Foner's
participation in, 94–95; parallels
between Reconstruction and, 104–
105; relationship of folklore and
popular culture to, 139; Naison
on activism and historical scholarship, 140–45
*Civil Rights Movement in America, The*
(University Press of Mississippi,
1986), 84
Clark, Mark, 55–56
Clark, Ramsey, 55–56
Clarke, John Henrik, 54
Class, socioeconomic: civil rights
movement and issues of, 13; Litwack on working-class experience, 17–18; Carter on Southern
culture and issues of, 37–42; and
black women's history, 63; Lewis
on black culture in mid-twentieth century, 70–71, 75; Lewis's
scholarship and paradigms of classism, 83, 84; Jones on small-town
culture and, 117–19, 120; Jones
on race relations and, 125
Colonialism: Lewis on African resistance to European, 85
Columbia University: graduate faculty of, in 1950s, 74–75
Commager, Henry Steele, 18
Commission on Interracial Cooperation, 5
Communist Party: blacklisting of
suspected members in 1940s, 92,
95; Naison on racial policies of,
in 1930s, 94, 143–45
*Communists in Harlem during the Depres-
sion* (Naison, 1983), 143–45
Cripps, Thomas, 122
Culture, American: Tindall on

influence of Jim Crow image on, 2–13; and Jewish immigrants in early twentieth century, 17–18; Litwack's examination of race relations and Southern, 24–28; Carter on race relations and Southern, 34–50; Hine's theory of black women's culture of dissemblance, 62; Lewis on class in mid-twentieth-century black, 70–71; Jones on small-town, 112–21, 128–30; political equality vs. cultural equality, 139. *See also* Popular culture

Currier, Ted, 72–73

Dabbs, James McBride, 42
Delaware Association for the Moral Improvement and Education of the Colored People, 123
DePillars, Murry N., 54
*Dictionary of American Biography*, 7
*Dispossessed: America's Underclasses from the Civil War to the Present, The* (Jones, 1992), 125, 137
Donald, David, 102
Douglas, Aaron, 26, 72, 89n.6
Douglass, Frederick, 94
Downey, Virtea, 60
Drake, St. Clair, 54
Dreyfus Affair: Lewis's research on, 81–82
Du Bois, W. E. B.: influence of, on development of black history, 16, 67, 139; and Litwack's research on Reconstruction, 19, 20; on racism and the black experience, 29–30, 31–32; Lewis's childhood memories of, 69, 70; Lewis's biography of, 85–86, 135; Foner's childhood memories of, 94; and Foner's view of Reconstruction, 103
Dunning, William A., 104

Edmonds, Helen, 67
Education, and race: in South during first half of twentieth century, 6–7; Jones on desegregation of, and small-town culture, 120. *See also* Segregation

Ellison, Ralph, 24, 28
Emmett, Dan, 3

Fanon, Frantz, 53–54
Fashoda incident of 1898: Lewis's interpretation of, 85
Fauset, Jessie, 70
Fink, Leon, 100
Fiske, John, 74
Fisk University: recording of experiences of former slaves in 1929, 23; faculty of, in 1950s, 72, 88–89n.6
Folklore: and achievement of social or cultural equality, 139
Foner, Eric: biography of, 91–92; on changes over time in approach to study of history, 92–110; personal experience and approach to race and history, 135–36; influence of, on Naison, 145
Foner, Jack D., 92, 95
Foner, Philip S., 92, 94
Fordham University: symposia on scholarship and race, xi–xii
Fox, Stephen, 68
France: Lewis's research on history of, 76–78, 134, 135
Franklin, John Hope: on integration of Southern research facilities, 7–8; influence of on Hine, 54, 56; and development of black history, 67, 139; as student at Fisk University, 73
Frazier, E. Franklin, 9
Freedom: Foner on ideological history of, in American context, 108–109
*Free Soil, Free Labor, Free Men* (Foner, 1970, 1995), 97–98, 135–36

Gatewood, Willard B., 70–71
Gautier, Mae, 43
Gender: bias in black history, 138
Genovese, Eugene, 67
Ghana: Lewis on teaching in, 78–79
*Gone with the Wind* (film), 21

151

Index

Index

phy of mid-twentieth century, 21;
evolution of Foner's scholarship
on, 101–108; Jones's study of
northern teachers of blacks in
Georgia during, 123–24
*Reconstruction: America's Unfinished Revolution, 1863–1877* (Foner, 1988),
105–106, 136
Religion: Jones on small-town culture and, 114–15
Resistance: black women and consciousness of, 62–63; and African
response to European colonialism, 85
Rice, Thomas Dartmouth "Daddy",
2–4
Richmond Reconstruction exhibit,
108
Roberts, Richard Samuel, 26
Robeson, Paul, 94
Rogers, Joel A., 70
Rudwick, Elliott, 67–68

Sambo: stereotype of, in American
tradition, 2
Sangnier, Marc, 77
Schrag, Oswald, 72
*Scottsboro: A Tragedy of the American South*
(Carter, 1969), 44, 45
Segregation: Jim Crow as eponym
for, 4; early history of, in South,
9, 11–13; Carter on Southern culture and, 37–42; and contemporary black separatism, 47; Jones
on small-town culture and,
119–20
Separatism, black: and segregation
in contemporary society, 47
Sexism: Hine on development of
black women's history and, 53–
64, 138
*Shelley v. Kramer* (1948), 58
Shenton, James P., 95–96, 145
Slavery: recording of experiences of
former slaves by Fisk University
in 1929, 23; examination of, in
Litwack's *Been in the Storm So Long*,
23–24; literature on aftermath of,
in British Empire and interpretation of Reconstruction, 103–104

Smelly, K. B., 76
Smith, Selden, 42
*Smith v. Allwright* (1944), 58
Smithsonian Museum: controversy
over exhibit on atomic bomb, 108
*Soldiers of Light and Love: Northern Teachers
and Georgia Blacks, 1865–1873*
(Jones, 1980), 124, 137
Soltau, Roger, 76
South: Tindall on influence of Jim
Crow image in, 4–13; reception
of Litwack's *North of Slavery* in
white press of, 21–22; Litwack's
examination of race relations and
culture of, 24–28; Carter on relations and white culture of, 34–50
South Africa: Foner on experience of
lecturing in, 109–10
*South Carolina Negroes, 1877–1900* (Tindall, 1952), 4
Southern Tenant Farmers' Union, 143
Spearman, Alice, 42–43
Spivack, Bernard, 72, 89n.6
Stampp, Kenneth M., 20
*State of Afro-American History, Past, Present, and Future, The* (Hine, 1986),
61–62
Stern, Fritz, 74
*Sweatt v. Painter* (1950), 58

Taylor, Alrutheus A., 8–9
Teachers and teaching: Litwack on
social justice and, 30–31; Foner
on black history and, 99–100;
Foner on experience of lecturing
in South Africa, 109–10; Jones's
study of northern teachers of
blacks in Reconstruction era Georgia, 123–24, 137
Thomas, Marcel, 81
Thompson, E. P., 98
Tillman, George, 8
Tillman, "Pitchfork" Ben, 8, 10
Tindall, George B.: biography of, 1–
2; on influence of Jim Crow image on history and race, 4–13;
influence of, on Carter, 45; personal experience and approach to
race and history, 132–33
Tobias, Channing, 69

Index

PAUL A. CIMBALA is Associate Professor of History at Fordham University in New York City. He is coeditor with Randall M. Miller of *American Reform and Reformers* and is author of the forthcoming *Under the Guardianship of the Nation: The Freedmen's Bureau and the Reconstruction of Georgia.* He is presently completing a book on black musicians in the nineteenth-century American South.

ROBERT F. HIMMELBERG is Professor of History at Fordham University, where he has been teaching since 1961 and has served in a number of capacities—as chair of the department, as President of the Faculty Senate, and since 1993 as Dean of the Graduate School of Arts and Sciences. Author of a number of articles and contributions to books, his best-known works are *The Origins of the National Recovery Administration: Business, Government and the Trade Association Issue, 1921–1933* and the edited series *Business and Government in America since 1870.*